Other titles in the A Retreat With... Series:

A RETREAT WITH MATTHEW

Going Beyond the Law

Leslie J. Hoppe, O.F.M.

ST. ANTHONY MESSENGER PRESS

Cincinnati, Ohio

Scripture citations are taken from the *New Revised Standard Version Bible*, copyright ©1989 by the Division of Christian Eductaiton fo the National Council of Churches of Christ in the U.S.A. and used by permission.

Cover illustration by Stever Erspamer, S.M.
Cover and book design by Mary Alfieri
Electronic format and pagination by Sandy L. Digman

ISBN 0-86716-329-1

Copyright ©2000, Leslie J. Hoppe, O.F.M.

Published by St. Anthony Messenger Press
www.AmericanCatholic.org
Printed in the U.S.A.

Contents

Introducing A Retreat With...

Twenty years ago I made a weekend retreat at a Franciscan house on the coast of New Hampshire. The retreat director's opening talk was as lively as a long-range weather forecast. He told us how completely God loves each one of us—without benefit of lively anecdotes or fresh insights.

As the friar rambled on, my inner critic kept up a *sotto voce* commentary: "I've heard all this before." "Wish he'd say something new that I could chew on." "That poor man really doesn't have much to say." Ever hungry for manna yet untasted, I devalued any experience of hearing the same old thing.

After a good night's sleep, I awoke feeling as peaceful as a traveler who has at last arrived safely home. I walked across the room toward the closet. On the way I passed the sink with its small framed mirror on the wall above. Something caught my eye like an unexpected presence. I turned, saw the reflection in the mirror and said aloud, "No wonder he loves me!"

This involuntary affirmation stunned me. What or whom had I seen in the mirror? When I looked again, it was "just me," an ordinary person with a lower-than-average reservoir of self-esteem. But I knew that in the initial vision I had seen God-in-me breaking through like a sudden sunrise.

At that moment I knew what it meant to be made in the divine image. I understood right down to my size eleven feet what it meant to be loved exactly as I was.

Only later did I connect this revelation with one granted to the Trappist monk-writer Thomas Merton. As he reports in *Conjectures of a Guilty Bystander*, while standing all unsuspecting on a street corner one day, he was overwhelmed by the "joy of being...a member of a race in which God Himself became incarnate.... There is no way of telling people that they are all walking around shining like the sun."

As an absentminded homemaker may leave a wedding ring on the kitchen windowsill, so I have often mislaid this precious conviction. But I have never forgotten that particular retreat. It persuaded me that the Spirit rushes in where it will. Not even a boring director or a judgmental retreatant can withstand the "violent wind" that "fills the entire house" where we dwell in expectation (see Acts 2:2).

So why deny ourselves any opportunity to come aside awhile and rest on holy ground? Why not withdraw from the daily web that keeps us muddled and wound? Wordsworth's complaint is ours as well: "The world is too much with us." There is no flu shot to protect us from infection by the skepticism of the media, the greed of commerce, the alienating influence of technology. We need retreats as the deer needs the running stream.

An Invitation

This book and its companions in the *A Retreat With...* series from St. Anthony Messenger Press are designed to meet that need. They are an invitation to choose as director some of the most powerful, appealing and wise mentors our faith tradition has to offer.

Our directors come from many countries, historical eras and schools of spirituality. At times they are teamed to sing in close harmony (for example, Francis de Sales, Jane de Chantal and Aelred of Rievaulx on spiritual friendship). Others are paired to kindle an illuminating fire from the friction of their differing views (such as Augustine of Hippo and Mary Magdalene on human sexuality). All have been chosen because, in their humanness and their holiness, they can help us grow in self-knowledge, discernment of God's will and maturity in the Spirit.

Inviting us into relationship with these saints and holy ones are inspired authors from today's world, women and men whose creative gifts open our windows to the Spirit's flow. As a motto for the authors of our series, we have borrowed the advice of Dom Frederick Dunne to the young Thomas Merton. Upon joining the Trappist monks, Merton wanted to sacrifice his writing activities lest they interfere with his contemplative vocation. Dom Frederick wisely advised, "Keep on writing books that make people love the spiritual life."

That is our motto. Our purpose is to foster (or strengthen) friendships between readers and retreat directors—friendships that feed the soul with wisdom, past and present. Like the scribe "trained for the kingdom of heaven," each author brings forth from his or her storeroom "what is new and what is old" (Matthew 13:52).

The Format

The pattern for each *A Retreat With...* remains the same; readers of one will be in familiar territory when they move on to the next. Each book is organized as a seven-session retreat that readers may adapt to their own schedules or to the needs of a group.

Day One begins with an anecdotal introduction called "Getting to Know Our Directors." Readers are given a telling glimpse of the guides with whom they will be sharing the retreat experience. A second section, "Placing Our Directors in Context," will enable retreatants to see the guides in their own historical, geographical, cultural and spiritual settings.

Having made the human link between seeker and guide, the authors go on to "Introducing Our Retreat Theme." This section clarifies how the guide(s) are especially suited to explore the theme and how the retreatant's spirituality can be nourished by it.

After an original "Opening Prayer" to breathe life into the day's reflection, the author, speaking with and through the mentor(s), will begin to spin out the theme. While focusing on the guide(s)' own words and experience, the author may also draw on Scripture, tradition, literature, art, music, psychology or contemporary events to illuminate the path.

Each day's session is followed by reflection questions designed to challenge, affirm and guide the reader in integrating the theme into daily life. A "Closing Prayer" brings the session full circle and provides a spark of inspiration for the reader to harbor until the next session.

Days Two through Six begin with "Coming Together in the Spirit" and follow a format similar to Day One. Day Seven weaves the entire retreat together, encourages a continuation of the mentoring relationship and concludes with "Deepening Your Acquaintance," an envoi to live the theme by God's grace, the director(s)' guidance and the retreatant's discernment. A closing section of Resources serves as a larder from which readers may draw enriching books, videos, cassettes and films.

We hope readers will experience at least one of those memorable "No wonder God loves me!" moments. And we hope that they will have "talked back" to the mentors, as good friends are wont to do.

A case in point: There was once a famous preacher who always drew a capacity crowd to the cathedral. Whenever he spoke, an eccentric old woman sat in the front pew directly beneath the pulpit. She took every opportunity to mumble complaints and contradictions—just loud enough for the preacher to catch the drift that he was not as wonderful as he was reputed to be. Others seated down front glowered at the woman and tried to shush her. But she went right on needling the preacher to her heart's content.

When the old woman died, the congregation was astounded at the depth and sincerity of the preacher's grief. Asked why he was so bereft, he responded, "Now who will help me to grow?"

All of our mentors in *A Retreat With...* are worthy guides. Yet none would seek retreatants who simply said, "Where you lead, I will follow. You're the expert." In truth, our directors provide only half the retreat's content. Readers themselves will generate the other half.

As general editor for the retreat series, I pray that readers will, by their questions, comments, doubts and decision-making, fertilize the seeds our mentors have planted.

And may the Spirit of God rush in to give the growth.

Gloria Hutchinson
Series Editor
Conversion of Saint Paul, 1995

Getting to Know Our Director

"Every scribe who has been trained in the kingdom of heaven is like the master of a household who brings out of his treasure what is new and what is old" (Matthew 13:52). Matthew wrote these words—they appear in none of the other gospels—and they are as close as we will ever get to knowing what Matthew thought of himself. Like a painter who includes a small self-portrait in a depiction of a crowd scene, the evangelist embeds this literary self-portrait in his story of Jesus. Still, we ask the question "Who was Matthew?"

The answer appears to be obvious: Matthew was a disciple of Jesus, one of the Twelve, and the author of the First Gospel. While each of the four lists of Jesus' Apostles includes the name Matthew (Matthew 10:2-4; Mark 3:16-19; Luke 6:14-16; Acts 1:13), the First Gospel, like the other three, is anonymous. The Gospels do not name their authors. A second-century Christian writer identified Matthew, one of the Twelve, as the author of the First Gospel and equated him with "Matthew the tax collector," whose call to follow Jesus is found in the First Gospel (see Matthew 10:3 and 9:9-13).

Was the Apostle Matthew, the former tax collector, the author of the First Gospel? It is possible—but not likely. The author of the First Gospel incorporated almost every verse of Mark's Gospel into his work. Is it probable that someone who accompanied Jesus throughout most of his ministry and was included among the Twelve had to rely on an account written by someone with no such connections? Shouldn't we expect the Apostle Matthew to rely on his memory in telling his story of Jesus? The answer is yes.

Mark also told the story of a tax collector's conversion at Capernaum (2:14-17), but the tax collector's name in Mark's Gospel is Levi—a name that never appears on any list of the Twelve. Luke (5:27-32) follows Mark's lead and names the tax collector Levi. Perhaps the author of the First Gospel changed the name of Levi to Matthew so that this former tax collector, whose call to follow Jesus is given such special notice, may be included among the Twelve.

Still, the phrase "the author of the First Gospel" is too cumbersome, so we will call our anonymous retreat master "Matthew." The anonymity of the evangelists is not difficult to appreciate. They were writing the story of Jesus and did not want to intrude into that story. However, each gospel writer left an individual stamp on his version of the Jesus story. Matthew's Gospel is a masterpiece that invites the willing reader to begin a journey with Jesus that starts in Bethlehem, moves to the Judean wilderness, then on to Galilee. After the Galilean ministry, Jesus begins his fateful trek to Jerusalem. There he completes his ministry before his crucifixion. Matthew concludes his Gospel by reporting the appearance of the Risen Jesus to his disciples in Galilee, commissioning them to take the Good News to all nations.

Our retreat master did not think of himself as a reformed tax collector but as a "scribe trained in the kingdom of heaven." He was not the master, teacher, rabbi—that was Jesus' role. Matthew was the scribe—that is, one schooled by the master who can then faithfully transmit the master's message. Still, Matthew is a bit too humble. In telling the Jesus story, Matthew shows himself to be a skilled teacher.

Placing Our Director in Context

If popularity is a measure of success, Matthew was very successful in telling his story of Jesus. The early Church held this Gospel in the highest esteem. Its preachers and theologians cited Matthew more often than any evangelist. Before the revision of the lectionary following Vatican II, Matthew's Gospel was the one read most often in the liturgy of the Church. Matthew was a skilled storyteller who has combined plot and characters in a way that engages any reader who wants to know "what sort of man" Jesus was (Matthew 8:27b).

Matthew himself was absolutely convinced that Jesus was the one sent by God to establish the reign of God in the final days as promised by the prophets of ancient Israel. The evangelist then presented Jesus as the fulfillment of his people's expectations ("Do not think that I have come to abolish the law and the prophets. I have come not to abolish but to fulfill" [Matthew 5:17]). But Matthew believed that Jesus was something more. He was also reinterpreter of those traditions ("You have heard that it was said to those of ancient times.... But I say to you...." [Matthew 5:21, 27, 33]). Matthew believed that Jesus was the fulfillment of ancient Israel's hopes but he fulfilled those hopes in a way that went beyond all expectations. Matthew's task then was to lay this truth out for his people.

Matthew begins his Gospel with a genealogy that serves to link Jesus with Abraham, David and the kings of Judah. Several times he notes that events in Jesus' life fulfill specific prophetic texts. For example, Matthew asserts that Jesus' healing of the sick was a fulfillment of Isaiah 53:4 (see Matthew 8:17). He also is familiar with the pious practices characteristic of early Judaism—almsgiving, prayer and fasting (see Matthew 6:1-18). Even the stinging critique of the Pharisees that Matthew places on Jesus' lips in chapter 23 show that Jesus' Jewish heritage was a central concern for Matthew. Similar unfavorable judgments on inauthentic and hypocritical religious leaders are also found in rabbinic literature. The harshness of Matthew's criticism of some Jewish religious leaders was likely the result of his frustration because most Jews who heard the proclamation of Jesus and the Gospel did not respond with faith and repentance. It was clear to Matthew that Jesus was the Messiah. Unfortunately, messianic expectations were not widespread among the Jews of Jesus' day. In fact, most religious leaders discouraged these expectations because they were potentially very dangerous. There were a few messianic pretenders, who succeeded in little else but rousing the ire of the Romans.

The Jewish community who produced the Dead Sea Scrolls did have highly developed hopes for the coming of at least two messiahs, but their influence over the majority of first-century Jews was negligible. Despite all this, Matthew wanted to share his beliefs about Jesus with his fellow Jews, inviting them to recognize in Jesus God's final and decisive intervention in the life of the Jewish community. Those Christians who have found support for the anti-Semitic ideology in Matthew are guilty of a gross misunderstanding of the evangelist's purpose. More than anything else, Matthew wanted to lead more Jews into the Christian community.

While Jesus' Jewish roots are important for Matthew, he concludes his Gospel by underscoring the universal scope of the Church's mission by having the risen Jesus commission his disciples to preach the gospel to "all nations" (Matthew 28:16-20). From the first pages of the Gospel, however, Matthew is preparing his readers for the inclusion of the gentiles. Jesus' genealogy includes four women, each of whom was a gentile (Tamar, Rahab, Ruth and Bathsheba; 1:3, 5-6) and the gentile magi who come to honor Jesus at his birth (2:1-12). Jesus responds to the faith of the Roman centurion in 8:5-13, heals the Gadarene demoniacs in 8:28-34, accedes to the request of the Canaanite woman in 15:21-28. Though Matthew acknowledges that Jesus directed his mission to Israel (10:5), he realizes that God intended to invite all people to the Kingdom.

Matthew makes his affirmations about the identity of Jesus, the purpose of his mission, the place of Jew and gentile in the Reign of God by telling a story. He begins with a genealogy, describes the unusual circumstances of Jesus' birth, relates what Jesus said and did in the course of his ministry, reports the events of Jesus' final hours, and tells of several appearances of the risen Jesus to his disciples. A large measure of Matthew's success as an evangelist is what he does in weaving together an intriguing plot and engaging characters.

The story begins with so much promise. A miraculous birth of a child destined to save his people offers readers hope. However, the life of the adult Jesus is marked by apparent failure. Opposition to him reaches a climax when the religious leaders of the community engineer his execution on trumped-up charges. What began with so much promise appears to have ended in tragedy. But no—Matthew's Gospel ends with the risen Jesus commissioning his disciples to carry on his mission.

A set of interesting characters carries the story to its triumphal conclusion. There is the perplexed Joseph, who takes Mary as his wife and agrees to act as the father to her child; and the maniacal Herod, who hears of the child's birth, considering it a threat to his rule. There is the band of Galilean peasants and fishermen who are attracted to Jesus and become his closest followers, but who never quite understand him and abandon him in his time of need—though they are rehabilitated in the end.

There are the scores of sick, sinners and the poor who find Jesus a source of hope in their lives. There are the Pharisees who are livid because of Jesus' popularity and his unwillingness to live by their standards of conduct. There are the priests and elders of Jerusalem who turn that city's people against Jesus and manipulate an irresolute Roman governor. There are the women who go to anoint Jesus' corpse but who meet the risen Christ instead.

The value of the story format chosen by Matthew and the other evangelists is that it engages the reader in a unique way. The reader cannot remain detached but is drawn into the dynamism of Matthew's plot. The evangelist leads the reader to encounter Jesus. The reader is more easily drawn into the mystery of the reign of God that Jesus announces.

Matthew did not create this technique of leading people to Jesus. Mark's Gospel was first and set a pattern for the others. Matthew's contribution to the gospel form is his lacing the narrative with sayings of Jesus. While he likely made use of earlier but now lost collections of Jesus' sayings, Matthew arranges these into speeches or sermons that can be easily integrated into his story. The best known of these is the Sermon on the Mount (Matthew 5—7).

Careful analysis of the Sermon on the Mount and other discourses in Matthew's Gospel have led to the conclusion that Matthew has not provided verbatim reports of what Jesus said to the crowds on specific occasions. It is more likely that the evangelist grouped sayings together by theme, or sometimes through wordplays and other literary techniques, and simply inserted these collections into his story at appropriate moments. The result of Matthew's efforts at assembling

Jesus' sayings into discourses is to give readers an experience of the effectiveness of Jesus' proclamation of God's reign. One feature of Matthew's portrait of Jesus is the authority, conviction and commitment evident in Jesus' preaching. For Matthew, Jesus is powerful in word.

The evangelist also portrays Jesus as powerful in deed. Jesus heals a leper (8:1-4), cures the centurion's servant at a distance (8:5-13), calms the waters of the Sea of Galilee stirred up by the winds (8:23-27). He casts out demons (8:28-34), brings a dead girl back to life (9:18-26), opens the eye of a blind man (9:27-31), loosens the tongue of a mute person (9:32-34). There was no way to measure Jesus' compassion toward those in need (9:36). Though he knew that the limits of time and space prevented him from reaching everyone, Jesus asked his disciples to pray that God send other laborers for the harvest (9:38).

One key to determining when Matthew wrote is to remember that he used the Gospel of Mark extensively. Mark composed his Gospel about A.D. 70. Allowing some time for Mark's Gospel to be spread about the Christian world so that Matthew could become acquainted with it, it is likely that Matthew wrote at least ten years after Mark. The community of Matthew was composed largely of Jews who had come to accept Jesus as the Messiah. The attention that Matthew gives to gentiles in his Gospel suggests that a significant number of gentiles were becoming part of that community.

The controversies in the Gospel regarding proper observance of the Law may reflect that there were some tensions in Matthew's community between Jewish and gentile Christians. The letters of Paul attest to the existence of such tensions in some of the places he evangelized, so we ought to expect them in Matthew's mixed community. The place where the First Gospel was composed could have been anywhere there was a mixed population of Jew and gentile. Quite a few cities in the eastern Mediterranean region fit that description.

These uncertainties aside, Matthew's purpose is clear enough. He wants to describe how a person ought to live in obedience to God in the days after the mission of Jesus. The Law of Moses speaks to the circumstances of another age. Matthew writes for believers who are living after God has offered the world salvation in Jesus Christ. He believed that he and his fellow Christians were living in the age foreseen by the prophets and longed for by the pious. For Matthew, however, living in this new age does not mean jettisoning the traditions of ancient Israel. That is why he sees himself as the "scribe who has been trained in the kingdom of heaven...who brings out of his treasure what is new and what is old" (Matthew 13:52).

DAY ONE
Walking With Jesus

Introducing Our Retreat Theme

The Hebrew word which refers to what we call ethics or morality is *halakah*. Literally, it means "walking." Matthew wanted to provide a new halakah—a new way of walking—for his community, which had a significant number of Jewish Christians. It was not enough for them to accept Jesus as the Messiah: "Not everyone who says to me, 'Lord, Lord,' will enter the kingdom of heaven..."(Matthew 7:21a). They had to lead a life worthy of the gospel: "Unless your righteousness exceeds that of the scribes and Pharisees, you will never enter the kingdom of heaven" (5:20). By telling the story of Jesus' words and deeds, Matthew shows his community how they must "walk."

During this retreat, we will follow Jesus and his disciples as they walk through Palestine, learning from our Master as we walk. We begin in Bethlehem and then go with the Holy Family to Egypt and finally Nazareth, where Jesus grew to adulthood. From Nazareth, we follow Jesus to the Judean wilderness where he met John the Baptist and confronted evil personified as he prepared to begin his mission. After his Baptism and temptation, Jesus walked back to Galilee. There he began teaching about the coming reign of God.

The reaction to Jesus was mixed. While people recognized that there was something unique about him, hostility mounted against him—hostility encouraged by religious leaders who saw Jesus as a challenge to their authority. In the end, Jesus' Galilean ministry proved to be unsuccessful and he cursed three towns, Chorazin, Bethsaida and Capernaum, where most of his ministry took place. Jesus then began a fateful journey with his disciples to Jerusalem.

He had no illusions about what awaited him in Jerusalem. Three times in the course of his journey south he predicted his violent death. He spoke to the Twelve about the cost of being his followers. Arriving in Jerusalem, Jesus began a short and intense ministry in that city. He had some difficult exchanges with his opponents and spoke in ominous terms about the judgments that awaited the city and the world.

During this retreat, we will retrace the journeys that Jesus took through Palestine as narrated by Matthew. At specific places, we will stop and listen to what Jesus is saying to us today. We prayerfully read the Gospel of Matthew because we believe that Jesus is speaking to us in those words crafted by the evangelist so long ago.

Opening Prayer

Loving God, you revealed yourself to the people of Israel through the words of their priests, prophets and sages. Then you revealed yourself to the whole world through Jesus. We ask you to be with us as we walk with the Lord Jesus through the land he called home. We want to hear him speak to us, call us, comfort us, challenge us, inspire us, heal us, lead us, teach us. Add your blessing to our prayerful reflections so that during this time of retreat

we can learn how to walk with you. We ask this through
Jesus, the Messiah, who lives and reigns now and forever.
Amen.

RETREAT SESSION ONE

Read Matthew 1:1—2:23. What strikes someone who
is reading Matthew's version of Jesus' infancy is what is
not there. There is no apparition of Gabriel to the Virgin
Mary, no journey by Mary from Nazareth to Judah to
assist Elizabeth in her final months of an unexpected
pregnancy. Joseph and Mary make no journey from
Nazareth to Bethlehem to be enrolled for the census.
There are no angels singing God's praises in the hearing
of shepherds who leave their flocks to see what the angels
are singing about. It seems that all of the most charming
features of the Christmas story are absent from Matthew.

Indeed, Matthew sets a more somber tone at the
beginning of his Gospel. The story of Jesus' birth and
infancy is a story of a plot born of fear and jealousy, the
murder of innocents, a flight to escape, years of exile and
then settlement in an obscure village. Still, Matthew
makes it clear that this Jesus brings the promise of God's
abiding presence with him.

Matthew begins with a family tree that binds Jesus to
his people—the people of Israel. Jesus is "the son of
David and son of Abraham." With that phrase alone,
Matthew tells us that it is impossible to appreciate who
Jesus was and what Jesus did without immersing
ourselves in the story of his people, their hopes, their
vision. Anyone who wants to learn how to "walk with the
Lord" must remember that Jesus, his disciples and the

vast majority of the people to whom he ministered were Jews. It is impossible to know Jesus while ignorant of the religious traditions that shaped him and his message.

"God-With-Us" in Bethlehem

The setting for the opening scene of Matthew's Gospel is presumably Bethlehem. While both Matthew and Luke agree that Jesus was born in Bethlehem, Luke explicitly states that Mary and Joseph were living in Nazareth prior to Jesus' birth, but Matthew does not mention Nazareth until long after Jesus is born. Joseph takes his family there because he was afraid of what might happen to Jesus were they to return to Bethlehem. His worst fears were confirmed by a dream in which he received a warning about those who might seek Jesus' life were they to know that he was alive.

This first scene (Matthew 1:18-25) introduces a young man named Joseph, distressed by what he has learned about Mary, the woman to whom he is engaged. She is pregnant with a child that Joseph knows is not his. Joseph decided that he could not go through with the marriage, but he did not permit his ego to determine his response to this troubling news. He could have insisted that Mary suffer the penalty reserved for adulterers, but decided instead on a quiet end to their relationship. Like his namesake, Joseph had a dream that changed his life. He dreamed that an angel told him that Mary's child was conceived through "the Holy Spirit" and that he was to take Mary into his home.

When the child was born, Joseph was to welcome it and give it the name "Jesus." Matthew is the one evangelist who underscores the significance of Jesus' name. The name *Jesus* is a Latinized form of the Hebrew name *Joshua*. It means "Yahweh helps" or "Yahweh saves." The angel, who instructs Joseph in the course of his dream, says that Mary's child is to have this name because he "will save his people from their sins" (1:21). In the rest of his Gospel, Matthew shows Jesus fulfilling the destiny foreshadowed by his name. Jesus saves people from the burdens that overwhelm them. He heals the sick, forgives sinners, welcomes social and religious outcasts. He urges his disciples to do the same. The very name that Joseph is to give Mary's child proclaims the purpose of Jesus' coming.

In reflecting on Jesus' approaching birth, Matthew cites Isaiah 7:14 and gives Jesus another name: "Emmanuel" (1:23). This Hebrew name means "God is with us." In citing the text from Isaiah, Matthew tells his readers not only that the birth of Jesus was part of a divine plan, but also that this Jesus was the way God has chosen to be with us. The attentive reader concludes that the child Joseph is to raise is not simply another prophet or religious teacher. Indeed, the humanity of Jesus is God's chosen means of being present in this world. That humanity did disclose the presence of God for some people, but for most people who encountered Jesus, his humanity served to conceal God's presence. Jesus, the Emmanuel, the God-with-us, does not pose the divine presence, but makes it available. Experiencing God in Jesus requires faith.

Matthew does not spend any time giving details of Jesus' birth. In the next scene of his story, he introduces the magi—gentiles who come to honor Jesus at this birth. At the very beginning of his Gospel, the evangelist stresses that the significance of Jesus' birth transcends Jewish messianic hope. The presence of the magi presages the risen Jesus' commission to take the gospel to all nations. Still, the more immediate role they play in Matthew's story is to occasion the first opposition that

Jesus will experience in his life. While Herod was not successful in destroying the child Jesus, eventually the chief priests and elders will succeed in persuading Pilate to execute the adult Jesus.

Herod the Great knew that he was not loved by his people. Augustus Caesar named him "king of the Jews." Many of his subjects regarded him as nothing more than a high-placed collaborator. Little wonder then that Herod was concerned about any potential rival. He took no chances and had many innocent children murdered because he thought one of them might take his throne. The third scene tells how Joseph's obedience to instructions he received in a second dream kept Jesus out of harm's way. The fourth scene is truly horrific. Still, Matthew asserts that even the slaughter of the innocents was the fulfillment of prophecy (Jeremiah 31:15). By their deaths, the children Herod massacred bore witness to the belief of the Christian community that Jesus was God's chosen one. The life of Jesus from the very beginning was the fulfillment of the Law and the Prophets.

Sheltered in Egypt

The Holy Family is forced to take refuge in Egypt to keep the child safe from Herod. Egypt was a logical choice. The Bible notes that others have escaped a monarch's anger there. Jeroboam, who led an unsuccessful revolt against Solomon, fled to Egypt (1 Kings 11:40). The prophet Uriah, a contemporary of Jeremiah, announced God's judgment against Judah and he had to flee to Egypt because of the king's anger at his words (Jeremiah 26:21). Jeremiah, too, was taken to Egypt by a band of conspirators who opposed Babylonian rule in Jerusalem (Jeremiah 43:8-13). Of course, the principal biblical image behind Matthew's story of the flight was the migration of Jacob and his family to Egypt during a famine in Canaan.

It was not difficult for Joseph to arrange Jesus' escape. There was a continuous stream of caravans between Palestine and Egypt. Joseph kept his family there until Herod the Great died. Again, Matthew sees a deeper significance beyond the mad actions of a despot and the fearsome flight of a young couple and the child. He sees Jesus' return to Palestine as a fulfillment of the prophecy, "Out of Egypt I have called my son" (Matthew 2:15, Hosea 1:11).

Settled in Nazareth

The final scene of Matthew's story of Jesus' birth and infancy takes place in an obscure village in Galilee. Matthew observes that Joseph settled his family in Nazareth because he feared that Archelaus, the son and successor of Herod the Great in Judea, would be not better than his father. The Romans divided Herod's kingdom among his surviving sons. Archelaus received Judea and the title "ethnarch," that is, "ruler of a nation." Archelaus inherited the worst features of his father's personality. His rule became so despotic and erratic that the Romans eventually deposed him and ruled Judea directly through a procurator. Joseph chose not to return to Bethlehem because it was in Judea. Joseph was afraid to return to Bethlehem, his hometown. He clearly did not want to expose Jesus to the jealous impulses of a paranoid ruler like Archelaus. Joseph chose to settle in a small village in central Galilee called Nazareth. Matthew asserts that this choice was the fulfillment of prophecy, though Joseph may have made his choice because Nazareth was near the city of Sepphoris, which was being rebuilt by Herod Antipas. This project afforded a great opportunity for a skilled workman like Joseph. The people of

Sepphoris revolted against Roman rule immediately following the death of Herod the Great in 4 B.C. The Romans put down the revolt with great ferocity. They killed the men, sold the women and children into slavery and leveled the city. When the Romans settled Herod's will, they divided his kingdom among his surviving sons, giving Galilee to Herod Antipas, who decided to rebuild Sepphoris and make it his capital. Settling in Nazareth kept Jesus far from Archelaus and gave Joseph an opportunity to support his family by working at Sepphoris.

Matthew ends his story of Jesus' birth and infancy by noting that Joseph's choice of Nazareth filled a prophecy: "(Joseph) made his home in a town called Nazareth, so that what had been spoken through the prophets might be fulfilled, 'He will be called a Nazorean'" (Matthew 2:23). Though there is some evidence that Nazareth was occupied before the time of Christ, the Old Testament never mentions the village. The text that Matthew quotes does not appear in any prophetic book and it is difficult to know what Matthew is referring to here. Perhaps Matthew is asserting that Jesus will be totally consecrated to God like the Nazirites of old (see Numbers 6:2-8).

Antipas modeled Sepphoris according to the pattern of other Hellenistic cities that were built in Palestine under the Greeks and Romans. It was a city with a population that approached thirty thousand, made up of Jews and Romans. Since Antipas made it his capital, it was home to the bureaucracy that administered Galilee. Antipas wanted to impress his Roman patrons so the city had an impressive commercial center with buildings adorned with striking mosaics, a theater, a council chamber, an archive, an aqueduct, Roman temples and a mint. Josephus, a first-century Jewish apologist, called it "the ornament of all Galilee." Jesus, then, grew to adulthood near this urban center. The Gospels never mention Sepphoris and, therefore, people do not associate it with Jesus or the rise of Christianity. It is unlikely, however, that Jesus could be immune from the influence of a large urban center so near to his home village. Nazareth was economically and politically dependent on Sepphoris, and the people of Nazareth no doubt felt the city's cultural influence as well.

Walking With the Lord

Matthew's story of Jesus' birth and infancy helps set the tone for the rest of the Gospel. The evangelist believed Jesus to be the Messiah, the descendant of David whom God had chosen to establish God's rule in this world. Still, the evangelist was painfully aware that most of his fellow Jews did not share this belief. Jesus failed to persuade them that the coming of the reign of God was imminent. The religious leadership of the Jewish community was united in opposing the message that Jesus was proclaiming. The priests, elders, scribes and Pharisees, with very few exceptions, remained unconvinced by Jesus. The circumstances of Jesus' birth portended the opposition that he was to experience in his ministry. The hesitancy of Joseph and the paranoia of Herod were just the beginning of a mission that was to end with Jesus' execution.

Despite the menacing circumstances of Jesus' birth, Matthew insists that God was present throughout. He makes this clear by his five citations of Old Testament prophecies in the first two chapters of his Gospel. The discerning eye can see the real presence of God in the events of Jesus' birth and infancy. The role of Jesus, according to Matthew, is clear from his very name. Jesus will bring salvation from sin. The salvation that Jesus will bring fulfills the deepest longings of ancient Israel but transcends them as well. While Jesus is the Messiah of Israel, he is also the savior of the world.

Ancient Israel's prophets directed people's attention to the future, which was to witness the decisive and final movement of God into their lives. This movement will establish God's rule in this world and fulfill people's hopes and dreams. However, Jewish religious tradition did not prepare people for the fulfillment that came through Jesus. Indeed, Jesus was the fulfillment of prophetic expectation as Matthew asserts. Still, this fulfillment went far beyond the expectations that the prophets encouraged. Unfortunately, early Jewish religious tradition was not malleable enough to integrate the ministry of Jesus with these expectations. The message that Jesus proclaimed sounded too "untraditional" to be true. While there were people like Joseph who were able to overcome their hesitancy, there were too many like Herod and the people of Jerusalem, who were troubled by the coming of Jesus.

To walk with Jesus along the way that begins in Bethlehem, Egypt and Nazareth requires us to be open to the Spirit who is calling us to broaden our horizons. Our religious traditions have brought us this far, but we need to hear what God is saying to us today. God is calling us to greater generosity, to a new level of commitment, to a closer relationship. To answer that call involves hearing God's word speaking to us in new circumstances and with greater urgency.

A retreat affords us the opportunity to consider prayerfully the shape our conversion is to take. What is God calling us to do with our lives? How have our experiences prepared us for this moment? When we read the Scriptures, what is God saying to us? Where do we go from here? The religious traditions that have shaped our lives of faith have prepared us to hear God calling us through Matthew's Gospel to a new level of commitment.

More than thirty years ago, Pope John XXIII recognized that God was calling for new Christian initiatives. He summoned the bishops of the world to an ecumenical council to help him lead the Church in this.

The Second Vatican Council has made it possible for Christians to respond to the gospel of Jesus Christ in new ways. For example, the council began a process of reconciliation to heal the divisions in the Church that resulted from the Reformation—divisions from the sixteenth century that remain today. From small-town ministerial associations to commissions made up of leading Protestant and Catholic theologians, the process of ecumenical dialogue, reconciliation and cooperation inspired by the council continues. Another important initiative has been reconciliation with the Jewish people. The council's repudiation of the notion that Jews were responsible for the death of Jesus has led to the Church's confessions and repudiation of the sin of anti-Semitism. Pope John Paul II went to pray in a synagogue in Rome and has led the Christian faithful in a new appreciation of the role of our "elder brothers and sisters" in God's plan of salvation.

The practical difficulty that Matthew had in convincing his fellow Jews that Jesus was the Messiah is that the Jewish religious community of the first century was a traditional society. In such a society, change does take place, but at a very measured pace. The preaching of Jesus called for people to make an immediate and decisive change in their lives. Jesus did not allow for half-measures or hesitation. This is what made it so difficult for his fellow Jews to accept him and his message.

Matthew tries to make it easier for his fellow Jews to accept the gospel. Five times in his story of Jesus' birth and infancy he notes that what happened was the fulfillment of prophecy. Despite this obvious concern to underscore Jesus' relationship to his ancestral traditions, Matthew suggests that Jesus' mission transcends Judaism. That is the significance of the magi's appearance.

The magi are not the only outsiders that appear in the infancy story. Matthew traces Jesus' genealogy through Joseph, although Joseph is not Jesus' biological father. Reflecting the patriarchal bias of his culture, Matthew lists Jesus' male ancestors almost exclusively, including only four women, none of whom were Israelites by birth. Tamar was a prostitute who helped the Israelite spies reconnoiter the city of Jericho before the Israelite attack and later married into the tribe of Judah (Joshua 2:1-21; 6:22-25). Ruth was from Moab—a land whose people were never to be admitted into the Israelite community (Deuteronomy 23:4). She, too, married into Judah and was the grandmother of David. The "wife of Uriah" was Bathsheba, the woman over whom David committed adultery and murder so that he could include her in his harem (2 Samuel 11:1—12:24). She later became Solomon's mother. These women become part of the Israelite story in unusual and even shocking ways.

The inclusion of these "outsiders" in the Jewish community and Matthew's mention of them in the genealogy of Jesus is a portent of what will happen during Jesus' ministry. What was so shocking to the good religious people of Jesus' day was his practice of associating with social and religious outcasts. Jesus sought the company of sinners in order to help them experience the saving love of God.

Matthew emphasizes that we need to think about the way God is present and active in the world in new ways. The people of Jesus' days were not always able to do this and missed their opportunity to recognize Jesus for who he was. Too many thought of him as misguided or even subversive. This time of retreat offers us an opportunity to reflect on God's presence and activity in our world.

While God is present in the ministry of the Church as it proclaims the gospel and administers the sacraments, can we see God's presence in other ways? What do we think of the struggles of people to be free from racial and ethnic prejudice? Can we see the presence of God in people oppressed by an unjust economic system? Do we see the Word of God being proclaimed when people are promoting the value of all human life? Do we see the face of Jesus in the undocumented alien, prisoners on death row, victims of hate crimes, people living with AIDS, abused children, compulsive gamblers, substance abusers? Perhaps we see these as social, economic and political issues that are beyond what we thought we would focus on during our retreat. But Matthew challenges us to reconsider. The cast of characters in Matthew's story of Jesus' infancy includes: a young man called to marry his fiancée pregnant with a child that is not his, a political tyrant, obtuse religious leaders, strangers from another country, innocent children made victims to a king's paranoia, a frightened family forced into exile. The plot deals with social prejudice, a politically inspired massacre and political asylum. He has to intersperse his narrative with biblical citations to convince the reader that the story he is telling is the fulfillment of prophecy. Apparently, the evangelist believed that this would not be obvious to most readers.

Though Matthew wrote his story within fifty years of Jesus' ministry, the characters and the plot of his first two chapters sound surprisingly current. Jesus' story then begins in the cross currents of social prejudice and political injustice. Why is it then, that some Catholics find the American bishops' pastoral letters on nuclear weapons and the economy unwarranted excursions into areas that are not the Church's concern? At the very least, walking with Jesus in Bethlehem, Egypt and Nazareth ought to lead us to reconsider what we believe "religion" to be. Matthew, our retreat master, will not allow us to withdraw into a type of spirituality that is totally consumed with matters of the interior life and personal morality—as important as these are. The conversion his Gospel calls us to is a conversion whose horizons are broader than that.

Retreatants who choose Matthew for their director know that they have to expand the frontiers of their conversion. Never again can conversion be a matter only of an interior response to the Word of God. That Word became incarnate at a real time, in a real place, among real people. The Incarnation makes every human concern an issue in the spiritual life.

Walking with Jesus means taking the Incarnation seriously.

For Reflection

- *Take time to reread Jesus' genealogy (Matthew 1:1-17). The opening line of the genealogy states that Jesus is "the son of David, the son of Abraham." What is the significance of this statement for Christians today? Recall particularly the women in Jesus' genealogy. What does their presence there mean to you?*

- *Reflect on Joseph, an important character in Matthew's story of Jesus' birth. Matthew tells us that he was afraid to take Mary as his wife, and afraid to return to Bethlehem even after Herod's death. What are you afraid of as you begin this walk with the Lord? What makes you hesitant and concerned in your efforts to give new shape to your life of conversion?*

- *The magi do not share the religious traditions of the Jews, yet they recognized the significance of Jesus' birth. Reflect on the magi. What significance do they have for your life with God?*

- Consider Herod and the massacre of the innocents. What led to Herod's decision to commit such a horrible crime? What role does this scene have in Matthew's overall conception of the story of Jesus' birth?

- *The Flight to Egypt was necessary to keep the infant Jesus safe from Herod. Does this episode shed any light on the problems of political and economic refugees today? How do you think Christians should respond to the phenomenon of migration in today's world?*

Closing Prayer

Gracious God, Jesus came into this world as a sign of your presence in and care for this world and all its people. Jesus came at a time when your people needed reassurance of your love for them. Still, some did not recognize him when he came—some were troubled rather than comforted at his coming. At the same time, something entirely unexpected happened. Gentiles—people who were not children of Abraham as Jesus was—came to offer him homage at his birth. Be with us during this time of retreat. Help us to feel your presence as we walk with Jesus, learning from him what you would have us do. Send your Spirit upon us so that we can act on the Word that is the source of our life and hope. We ask this through Jesus, the Lord. Amen.

DAY TWO
Who Is This Man, Jesus?

Coming Together in the Spirit

People devote a lot of time and money to "find themselves." Psychiatrists, counselors and psychologists commit themselves to years of difficult professional training to help people understand who they are. Sometimes unraveling a person's identity can be bewildering.

Accounts of some extreme cases like *The Three Faces of Eve* describe how an individual can develop multiple personalities, making self-understanding an almost impossible goal. But even when serious pathology is not an issue, arriving at self-understanding is always a process.

If self-knowledge is so difficult to attain, how can we come to know another? How can we penetrate the barriers that personal expectations, prejudice, misunderstanding, stereotypes and, paradoxically, over-familiarity place in the way of knowing another? Add to these the distance of time and culture and we can appreciate the task we set for ourselves when we want to answer the question "Who is this man...?" about Jesus of Nazareth. Still, no person—especially no Christian—can ignore this question. The person of Jesus is the central focus of Christian belief. This is the goal we have for today—answering for ourselves the question: "Who is this man...?" For only by answering that question can we understand who we are as believers.

Defining Our Thematic Context

Since Matthew wanted to preserve the Jewish character of the Christian movement, he had to be very careful in helping his readers comprehend the person of Jesus. Certainly, the claims that the first Christian community made about Jesus were the primary reason for the rabbis to question the "Jewishness" of the Christian movement. Still, Matthew could not compromise the Christian confession about Jesus.

The evangelist carefully crafted his portrait of Jesus. His stories provide a color and texture that no bald theological statements can match. The climactic development of his narrative leads the reader to an emotional affirmation of faith or an equally emotional rejection. Matthew does not allow his readers to remain neutral about Jesus.

Today we are going to reread some of what Matthew wants to say about Jesus. Our purpose is to strengthen our commitment of faith in Jesus as God's Word to us—a Word that is spoken directly and personally to each of us. It is a Word that calls us to faith, repentance, discipleship. It speaks to us of God's dominion over this world. It calls us to obedience and to mission as we await God's final coming into our world.

Opening Prayer

Let us pray. Gracious God, you spoke to us through ancient Israel's priests, prophets and sages and now you speak through Jesus, the Christ. Open our minds so that we can hear what you have to say to us this day. Touch our hearts so that, after hearing your word, we may be ready to act on it. Help us to hear Jesus' call to repentance, faith and discipleship. Empower us for the mission of making disciples of all nations. Be with us as we await Jesus' return when he will present a renewed world to you—a world that will witness the triumph of your justice and peace. We ask this through Jesus Christ, your Son and our Lord. Amen.

Retreat Session Two

How did most of Jesus' contemporaries experience him? How would they describe him?

The first word that would come to mind is "teacher" or perhaps "rabbi." Matthew presents Jesus as a teacher in the discourses of his Gospel—particularly in the Sermon on the Mount (chapters 5-7). Jesus acts like other Jewish teachers of his day. He gathers a group of disciples (students) around himself and teaches them his understanding of Torah. Matthew has Jesus call himself "a teacher" (23:8; 26:18) and describes the people as being astounded by differences between Jesus' teaching and that of other rabbis (7:29).

Still, Matthew makes it clear that seeing Jesus merely as a teacher and nothing more is to misunderstand him. In Matthew's Gospel, those who address Jesus as "rabbi" or "teacher" are those who do not understand him or prove to be his enemies. The only disciple to address Jesus as "rabbi" is Judas (26:25; 28:49). Those who either address Jesus as "teacher" or speak of him as such are Pharisees, Sadducees, scribes or lawyers. None of those who use this title to address Jesus are particularly sympathetic toward him. Indeed, usually they are looking for an opportunity to expose him as unqualified and therefore incompetent to teach. While Matthew presents Jesus as a teacher, he wants us to know that this is not the whole story.

If Jesus is someone more than just a teacher, who is he? When Jesus asks his disciples who people say he is (16:15), they suggest that people think of him as a prophetic figure:

> [Jesus] asked his disciples, "Who do people say that the Son of Man is?" And they said, "Some say John the Baptist, but others Elijah, and still others Jeremiah or one of the prophets." (16:13-14)

Some Jewish expectations about the future had an important place for a prophet of some sort. These expectations were fueled by those who read Malachi 4:5 as implying that the prophet Elijah was to return just before the days of the Messiah. Some bystanders at the crucifixion misunderstood Jesus' final words ("*Eli, Eli lema sabachthani*" [27:46]) and thought that he was calling for Elijah. Matthew, of course, identified John the Baptist as Elijah (11:14). Others read Deuteronomy 18:15, which speaks of God's raising up a prophet like Moses, as predicting that a second Moses was to come before God's final intervention on Israel's behalf. The Samaritan community, in particular, envisioned the future of Israel as the People of God as the work of a new Moses. They called him "the restorer." The place of the prophets in early Judaism was becoming more important. Their works were being set alongside the books of Moses. Jesus himself spoke of "the law and the prophets" (5:17). The ascendency of prophetic literature was due in part to the transformation of early Judaism into a religion based on ethics. Of course, the prophets were the great exponents of traditional Israelite morality.

Like the prophets before him, Jesus was destined to be rejected by Israel (23:34-39). Still, Matthew considered understanding Jesus as a prophet to be just as unsatisfactory as considering him to be just a teacher. Jesus is a prophet but he is certainly more than a prophet. Matthew asserts that the prophets point to Jesus (5:17; 11:13; 12:18). Jesus' ministry is the fulfillment of prophetic expectations about the future. Similarly, Jesus is not simply a prophet like Moses; he is someone far greater than Moses. He cites his own authority to have his disciples go beyond the Law of Moses (5:27-28). For Matthew, Moses and the prophets provide an important framework for understanding Jesus.

Beyond his identity as teacher and prophet, Matthew presents Jesus as "the Christ, the Messiah." The evangelist uses "Jesus Christ" as a double name (1:1, 18). He implies that some people believed Jesus to be "the Messiah" (27:17-22). The term "Christ" (messiah) is clearly important for Matthew. While Mark uses it only seven times, it appears thirty-nine times in Matthew. Messianic expectations among Jews of Jesus' day were not very strong except among the Jews of the Qumran community. The word *messiah* appears in only four of the many early Jewish religious writings that are not found in the Bible. Again, Qumran is the exception. Writings produced by the community at the Dead Sea envision at least two messiahs: one royal and the other priestly. Because the Qumran community was largely made up of disaffected priests, the priestly messiah had the pre-eminent position.

Since Matthew wanted to stress that Jesus is the fulfillment of God's promises to David (see 2 Samuel 7), presenting Jesus as the Christ, the Messiah, is essential for Matthew. It is an obvious attempt to underscore the Jewish matrix of the Christian movement.

The importance of the title *messiah* for Matthew can lead to the supposition that messianic expectations among Jews of Jesus' day were high. If we consider the data from Jewish religious texts of the time, we come to a different conclusion. Messianic expectations were not widespread. It may be that the leadership of the Jewish community in Roman Palestine did not want to stir up popular sentiment against Rome by speaking about an ideal Davidic king who was to restore Israel's political fortunes. Clearly, the Jews were in no position to challenge Roman rule as they found out during the failed revolt that took place about a decade before Matthew wrote his Gospel.

"Messiah" is a technical term referring to the ideal figure of the future, "the son of David" who will inaugurate God's rule on earth. From the very beginning of his Gospel, Matthew wants us to know that Jesus is the Messiah, the Son of David, the king of the Jews as foreseen "by the prophet" [Micah] (2:1-6). At the same time, the evangelist shows that the title Messiah, despite its connections with traditions about David and his descendants, can be misunderstood. When the magi came to Jerusalem inquiring about the "new-born king of the Jews" (2:2), Herod thought of the child as a potentially dangerous political opponent who had to be eliminated at all costs.

Peter confesses Jesus to be the Messiah. Though Jesus asserts that God made it possible for Peter to recognize Jesus as the Messiah, still he orders the disciples to say nothing about it to anyone.

Matthew underscored Jesus' identity as the "Son of David"—especially in the stories about healing. In Matthew's story of Jesus' passion, Pilate implies that people called Jesus the Messiah. Still, the priests and elders of Jerusalem, who handed Jesus over to Pilate, successfully persuade the people of the city to call for Jesus' execution despite his being known as the Messiah. The story of the Passion is full of ironic allusions to Jesus' messianic character: the Roman soldiers mock Jesus by hailing him as "king of the Jews" (27:29); the charge placed on the cross read, "This is Jesus, the King of the Jews" (27:37); the priests, elders, and scribes of Jerusalem mock the dying Jesus by asserting "He is the King of Israel" (27:42); some bystanders mistook Jesus' final words as calling for Elijah, who was to be the Messiah's precursor.

In effect, Matthew asserted that Jesus could be understood only in terms of Jewish expectations about the future. These expectations were evident at his birth, during his ministry, and in his final hours. Still, Matthew implies that understanding Jesus solely in messianic terms is to misunderstand him. Herod did not recognize Jesus for who he was but saw him only as a potential rival for political power. Jewish religious teachers successfully persuaded the people of Jerusalem that messianic claims made on Jesus' behalf were mere illusion. Yet, Matthew asserted that Peter, the first of the disciples to call Jesus "the Messiah," did so because he received a revelation from God. But while Jesus was the Messiah, he was something more.

A dramatic moment in the Gospel comes in the account of Jesus' trial before the Jewish court when the high priest asks Jesus to state, under oath, whether he is the Messiah. Jesus replies by speaking of himself as "the Son of Man" who will return enthroned at the right hand of God to administer the final judgment. The high priest takes this answer to be affirmative, though Jesus does not call himself "messiah" but "Son of Man." Though Matthew considered "messiah" an appropriate title for Jesus, he recognized that Jesus fulfilled Jewish messianic expectations in a way that transcended these expectations. Yes, Jesus is the messiah but a messiah who suffers in obedience and will return to judge the world as "the Son of Man."

Jesus was a teacher, a prophet, the new Moses, and the Messiah. Still, he was something more. But who was Jesus? Matthew has not one, but two, answers to that question. Jesus is Son of God *and* Son of Man. When Matthew uses the title "Son of God" in the story of Jesus' birth, he is underscoring Jesus' origin and unique relationship with God. He tells the story of Jesus' ministry to show that Jesus relives the story of ancient Israel, but as the obedient servant who shows that he is both the genuine Son of God and the true Israel by doing the will of God. Twice during Jesus' ministry God reveals him as the divine Son of God: at Jesus' Baptism and at the Transfiguration. The disciples who witness Jesus' calming of the sea confess him as the Son of God, as does Peter when Jesus asks what people think of him. This title appears in the story of Jesus' passion and redefines divine sonship as obedience to the point of death.

However, Jesus does not speak of himself as "the Son of God." The one title that Jesus regularly uses to speak of himself is "the Son of Man." This title, however, raises more questions about Jesus than it answers. There is no phrase in the Bible that has attracted more attention from scholars than "the Son of Man." It both reveals and conceals. It points to Jesus' role in God's plan to establish divine rule on earth, but it keeps Jesus hidden behind a mysterious cloud. People know that when Jesus speaks of "the Son of Man" he is referring to himself. Still, it is clear that not everyone accepts the theological implications that Jesus attaches to this phrase.

Jesus was not the first to use the phrase, "the Son of Man." It is a Semitic expression that can be indefinite as "someone," though it is clear that Jesus has a more definite referent in mind when he uses this expression to speak of himself. In the Book of Ezekiel, God addresses the prophet as "son of man" almost one hundred times. In those prophetic oracles, the expression emphasizes the prophet's lowly status before the all-holy God. In the poetry of the Old Testament, this expression usually means "a human being," though Psalm 8:4-5 gives a high status to human beings and has God crown "the son of man" like a king.

The most developed and exalted usage of this phase in the Old Testament occurs in the Book of Daniel. There "the Son of Man" is a human-like figure carried aloft by the clouds. Early Jewish and Christian theological speculation transformed Daniel's son of man into a transcendent agent of God's judgment and salvation which will become manifest during the last days of this world. Early Jewish literature uses this term to speak of a figure that combines traditions about the Davidic king (messiah), the servant of the Lord in Isaiah, and the eschatological figure of Daniel. The social setting evident when this term appears in Jewish literature is persecution and suffering. Jesus was preaching when these Jewish literary traditions that used "the Son of Man" were in circulation. It is unlikely that when Jesus used "the Son of Man" to speak of himself that he meant simply "I" or "me." The expression as it came to be used in early Jewish religious literature would not allow such a neutral meaning.

Matthew's use of "the Son of Man" reflects the

mysterious usage of this title. It can have one of three meanings, depending on the context. First, "the Son of Man" is the lowly servant of God: "Foxes have dens, and birds of the sky have nests, but the Son of Man has nowhere to rest his head." Second, Matthew's "Son of Man" is one who will suffer the indignities of the passion, give his life, but be raised from the dead: "The Son of Man is to be handed over to men, and they will kill him, and he will be raised on the third day." Matthew adopts this usage from the sources that he used in the preparation of his Gospel. "The Son of Man" image looks to the past: Jesus' ministry and his passion, death and Resurrection.

The evangelist, however, also uses this title when he looks to the future—and this is Matthew's special contribution. He uses this title when he wishes to speak about Jesus' exaltation in heaven and his role of a judge on the last day: "For the Son of Man is to come with his angels in the glory of his Father, and then he will repay everyone for what has been done."

The most familiar illustration of Matthew's association of the Son of Man with the final judgment is a parable that occurs only in the First Gospel: the parable of the sheep and the goats. According to this parable, the Son of Man will judge all peoples on the basis of their good deeds. These alone make it possible for people to possess eternal life. The sheep do not even have to recognize the presence of Christ in those they serve; they need only to be compassionate to those in need. This parable shows the extent Matthew is prepared to go in emphasizing the importance of good deeds. Here is the key to Matthew's presentation of Jesus in his Gospel. Although the evangelist uses many titles for Jesus, he was much more concerned that his readers serve the needs of the poor than that they should be correct in their understanding of who Jesus is. What does it matter if one confesses Jesus to be the messiah and Son of God if one does not obey Jesus? For Matthew, Christianity, like Judaism, is to be a system of "right doing" rather than a system of "right thinking."

Since the restoration following the return from the Exile, Judaism was evolving into a religion whose central focus was ethics. A most significant moment in this process was the publication of the Book of Deuteronomy in its final form. Deuteronomy is the text that marks the transition from the religion of ancient Israel to the religion of early Judaism. The former was the national religion of the Israelites. Its goals were the protection of the national state and dynasty and insuring of the fertility of the land. It achieved these goals through the maintenance of a sacrificial cult at Jerusalem and at other shrines in the land. Early Judaism was developing into a religion of individual salvation that could be achieved through obedience to a written, authoritative law. Obedience to that law brought blessing and disobedience brought a curse. Of course, this transition took several hundred years and Matthew wrote toward the end of it.

The problem that Jesus and the early Christians had with the development of Judaism into a religion based on an explicit ethical system was an innovation that Jesus regarded as unwarranted: the oral law of the Pharisees, or what Matthew called "the tradition of the elders" (15:3). This oral law was a body of traditional interpretations of the written law found in the Bible. Later rabbis described the goal of the "traditions of the elders" as "putting a fence around the (written) law." The Pharisees believed that all ancient Israel's misfortunes were the result of the people's disobedience. Moses laid a choice before all Israel:

> See, I have set before you today life and prosperity,
> death and adversity. If you obey the commandments
> of the LORD your God that I am commanding you
> today, by loving the LORD your God, walking in his
> ways, and observing his commandments, decrees,
> and ordinances, then you shall live and become
> numerous, and the LORD your God will bless you in
> the land you are entering to possess. But if your
> heart turns away and you do not hear, but are led
> astray to bow down to other gods and serve them,
> I declare to you today that you shall perish....
> (Deuteronomy 30:15-18)

To keep Israel from experiencing the effects of
disobedience one more time, the Pharisees developed the
prescriptions of the oral law, believing that this oral law
"protected" the written law from violation. If people kept
the oral law, they would never violate the written law and
thus would enjoy the blessings that come to the obedient.
Thus, the Pharisees believed that they were making it
possible for Israel to live in conformity to God's will.

The Pharisees maintained that this oral law was a
legitimate development of the written law and so
ascribed it to Moses. More important, they considered the
oral law just as binding as the written Torah. Jesus did
not. Consider the healing of the man with the withered
hand. The written law forbids work on the Sabbath (see
Exodus 20:8-11; Deuteronomy 5:12-15). Of course, it is
impossible to avoid all activity on the Sabbath so the
question naturally arose about what type of activity
violated the law. The presence of Jesus and a man with a
withered hand in the same congregation assembled for
Sabbath prayers led Jesus to question the Pharisaic
interpretation of the Sabbath commandment.

The Pharisees considered essential activity on the
Sabbath as permissible. For example, one could save a
person's life on the Sabbath. But they believed that

ailments that did not threaten life must be dealt with after the Sabbath. Jesus did not agree. Jesus did not regard the healing of the man's withered hand as a violation of the law. According to the Pharisees, one could rescue a sheep that fell into a pit on the Sabbath, so Jesus concluded that helping a human being should be all the more permissible. Jesus healed the man. His action was a threat to the Pharisaic system because of the high regard people had for Jesus. Matthew noted that the differences between Jesus and the Pharisees about the oral law were not simply polite discussions. He remarks that after the healing, the Pharisees "took counsel against (Jesus) to put him to death."

Though Jesus rejected "the tradition of the elders" as authoritative, he never once violated any law found in the written Mosaic tradition. Matthew made it clear that Jesus did not come "to abolish the law...but to fulfill." Jesus did not accept the theory of an authoritative oral law, but he taught that "not the smallest letter or the smallest part of a letter will pass from the law until all things have taken place." Those who teach otherwise will be called "least in the kingdom of heaven."

There is a problem with a religion based on a written law. It is the problem of minimalism. Many people will wonder about what is the least they can do and still fulfill their obligations. Such people do not ask "What more can I do?" but "What do I have to do?" That is why Jesus tells his disciples: "[U]nless your righteousness exceeds that of the scribes and Pharisees, you will never enter the kingdom of heaven." In the Sermon on the Mount, Jesus gives several examples of how his followers were to go beyond the commandments. The Law forbids killing, but Jesus calls his disciples to avoid anger and to seek reconciliation. The Law forbids adultery, but Jesus calls his followers to avoid even placing themselves in danger of committing such a sin. The Law allows for divorce, but Jesus calls for lifelong commitment. The Law permits retaliation when one is offended, but Jesus tells his followers "Do not resist an evildoer." Jesus wants his disciples to consider the written Law as a starting point rather than as a goal.

Matthew, then, wanted to preserve the genius of early Judaism—a religion whose foundation was an enlightened moral code that called for love of God and neighbor. When asked to name the greatest commandment in the Law, Matthew has Jesus state:

"You shall love the Lord your God with all your heart, and with all your soul, and with all your mind." This is the greatest and the first commandment. And a second is like it: "You shall love your neighbor as yourself." On these two commandments hang all the law and the prophets. (22:37-40)

The rest of early Judaism's moral code was simply an elaboration of these two commandments. Jesus, however, rejected the Pharisees' theory of an oral law, even though the Pharisees were well-intentioned in developing it. The problem is that "putting a fence around the law" sometimes led to minimalizing and trivializing the law. Indeed, following "the traditions of the elders" made it possible to evade one's moral obligations:

And why do you break the commandment of God for the sake of your tradition? For God said, "Honor your father and your mother," and "Whoever speaks evil of father or mother must surely die." But you say that whoever tells father or mother, "Whatever support you might have had from me is given to God," then that person need not honor the father. So, for the sake of your tradition, you make void the word of God. (15:3-6)

The parables in chapter 25 that have judgment as a theme (the ten virgins, the talents, the sheep and goats) appear to emphasize reward and punishment as the motive for moral conduct. Indeed, Judaism, Christianity and all religions with a strong moral code assume that God will reward those who live by that code and punish those who do not. Jesus instructs his disciples to pray, fast, and give alms in secret so that they will be rewarded by God. The beatitudes (5:3-12) each promise a reward. But we think of reward as an unworthy motive for actions. Of course, Matthew believed that God's rewards are always greater than we deserve. All of us are in the position of the workers in the parable who receive a full day's wage for just one hour's work. God always remains one who gives gifts rather than one who rewards merit. Still, Jewish tradition emphasizes that the commandments ought to be kept for their own sake and not for any advantage to be gained by obedience. In citing Deuteronomy's command to love God as the greatest of the commandments, Jesus makes it clear that it is love that motivates his followers. The rewards that Jesus promises in the gospel are for a life of abandonment to God, self-forgetfulness and service to our brothers and sisters.

As Christianity slipped farther from its Jewish moorings, ethics took a second place to dogmatics. Theological questions rather than moral ones became important. In the first few centuries of the Church's existence, Christians debated each other about a question that was central to Matthew's Gospel: "Who is this man Jesus?" Instead of framing an answer out of Jewish expectations about God's final movement in Israel's life, gentile Christians began using categories drawn from the Greek philosophical tradition. In place of titles like "the Son of Man," "the Messiah," "the Son of God," terms such as "person," "being," "essence" became the currency used in the attempts to understand Jesus. These terms had to be used with extreme precision. Anything less meant heresy.

Christianity soon became a religion of "right thinking" with dogmas that were to be formulated with great care and adhered to with great tenacity. One consequence of this concern for "right thinking" was the fragmentation of the Christian community. It began with the questions about the person and work of Jesus. Arians, Nestorians, docetists, monophysites are some of the strange names that Christians gave to one another in the course of the controversies about Christ. Does the Holy Spirit proceed from the Father and the Son as Western Christianity holds, or from the Father alone as Orthodox Christianity holds?

Since the sixteenth century, Western Christianity has fragmented itself into hundreds of ecclesial communities, each claiming to be the depository of authentic Christian tradition. This concern for doctrinal purity continues in the Roman Catholic Church, whose leadership looks with suspicion on every possible departure from magisterial teaching.

Matthew's Gospel suggests that we reassess our priorities in the following of Christ. The evangelist underscores the significance of "doing" rather than "thinking" when he has Jesus say: "Not everyone who says to me, 'Lord, Lord,' will enter the kingdom of heaven, but only the one who does the will of my Father in heaven" (7:21).

Jesus cares less what the disciples think of him and more about how they live in obedience to the divine will. Of course, this does not mean that the Christian theological tradition is a dispensable part of the Church's life. However, the gospel is not to be distilled for doctrines, but lived in fulfillment of God's will.

Matthew was not indifferent to what we think of as doctrinal concerns. His Gospel is a testimony to his belief that Jesus was miraculously conceived by the Holy Spirit in the womb of the Virgin Mary in fulfillment of Old Testament prophecy. He believed that the Holy Spirit descended on Jesus at his baptism by John in the Jordan. This empowered him to perform miracles that were signs of God's final and decisive movement in Israel's life. Matthew tells the story of Jesus' final hours to make it clear that the death of Jesus was a sacrifice through which God made a new and eternal covenant with humankind. Matthew also believed that Jesus was raised from the dead and given authority from God to rule over the universe. Finally, Matthew was convinced that Jesus was going to return to this world soon to exercise his divine authority in the final judgment. But above all, Matthew presents Jesus as one who calls people to follow him. He makes the most radical claim upon human beings that is possible. His claim upon us is total and absolute. Jesus demands that we give up our lives for him:

> If any want to become my followers, let them deny themselves and take up their cross and follow me. For those who want to save their life will lose it, and those who lose their life for my sake will find it. For what will it profit them if they gain the whole world and forfeit their life? Or what will they give in return for their life? (16:24-26)

This is not a call for martyrdom. Jesus does not necessarily want his disciples to die for him but to live for him.

The gospel is not a theological system but a way of life. It calls for a commitment to the ideals of Jesus Christ who, as Son of Man, will return as judge. Jesus is the teacher and rabbi who gathers a group of disciples to instruct them about fulfilling the divine will. He can speak with authority because he comes to his disciples as the "Son of God." But Jesus does more than speak. He fulfills his destiny as the messiah by living a life of obedience—obedience that led to the cross. Yes, Jesus is teacher, rabbi, prophet, Son of God, messiah and Son of Man. He fulfills all the diverse expectations of ancient Israel and early Judaism regarding the final intervention of God in the life of the people. He comes to call people to obedience—an obedience that encompasses the Torah that calls believers to love God and to love their neighbor.

Matthew's portrait of Jesus underscores the basic simplicity of the gospel message. There is no substitute for "good deeds." The message of Jesus is not about mystical prayer, enthralling liturgy, persuasive argumentation, great miracles, peace of conscience, logical systems of thought. In the Gospel Jesus calls his disciples to do "good deeds." The gospel, then, is a way of life—a life of love for God and neighbor. Everything else is dispensable. Early Judaism learned this from the bitter experience of the ancient Israelites, who sought to substitute almost anything from an elaborate Temple ritual to the search for wisdom. Qoheleth's verdict on these attempts is as concise as it is accurate: It is a vanity and a chase after the wind (see Ecclesiastes 1:2, 17). Jesus assembles a small group of disciples and instructs them in "good deeds." It is as simple as that.

Matthew's Jesus tells us that our righteousness must exceed that of the scribes and Pharisees. He challenges us to go beyond the commandments. He warns us about the impending judgment. He presents Jesus as a model of one so committed to the divine will that even suffering and death did not keep him from obedience. Matthew used several Jewish titles to speak of Jesus. He explicitly cited several prophetic texts that he believed were fulfilled by Jesus. The evangelist did not look at Christianity's Jewish matrix simply as a vehicle for understanding. He believed that Jewish religious tradition ought to be maintained among those Jews who confess Jesus to be the messiah and even among those gentiles who were coming into the Christian community:

> Amen, I say to you, until heaven and earth pass away, not the smallest letter or the smallest part of a letter will pass from the law, until all things have taken place.
> Therefore, whoever breaks one of the least of these commandments, and teaches others to do the same, will be called least in the kingdom of heaven; but whoever obeys and teaches them will be called great in the kingdom of heaven. (Matthew 5:18-19)

A most significant part of the Jewish matrix of Christianity was early Judaism's transformation into a religion of individual salvation based on obedience to a written authoritative law. For Matthew, obedience to Jesus' teaching was far more important than knowing precisely who Jesus was. No single title or combination of titles can adequately explain who Jesus is. What is more important is putting into practice what Jesus taught.

For Reflection

- *Why does Matthew imply that for the disciple "right doing" is more important than "right thinking"?*

- *In your assessment of your own Christian life, what is more important: "doing" or "thinking"? Do you think of Christian doctrines as motivating you to action in service of your sisters and brothers? Why or why not?*

- *What is your primary motive as you try to live the ideals of Jesus today?*

Closing Prayer

Loving God, Jesus, the Messiah, became obedient to death—even to death on the cross. We ask for the gift of the Spirit to empower us for the service of our sisters and brothers in need so that we can live in obedience to Jesus. He calls us to be forgetful of self as we give ourselves in loving service to you and our sisters and brothers. He promises eternal life to those who live not for themelves but for others. May our lives be worthy of the gospel we profess and may they be worthy of the future you have in store for those who love you and live in obedience to the gospel of Jesus, your Son and our Lord. Amen.

DAY THREE
Hastening the Kingdom

Coming Together in the Spirit

Many people look upon the problems of the British royal family with amusement, sympathy or perhaps even disdain. Why do the British people support the life-style of their royals? For most people today, monarchy is little more than an anachronism. We believe that political power derives from the people, who freely consent to invest officials whom they elect with that power for specific periods. The divine right of kings is an idea whose time is long past. With the ideology of the monarchy gone, why keep up the pretense of royal authority and power? Still, the resplendent glitter and pomp of royal ceremony are very reassuring to some people. They are willing to pay the price for that reassurance.

Monarchy, however, was an essential institution in the world of the Bible. When Jesus spoke about the mission that he received from God, he used a metaphor derived from the experience of monarchy: the kingdom of heaven. Appropriating this metaphor has never been easy for Christians—least of all in our day when monarchy as a political system has been consigned to the margins of modern thought. We need to remember that monarchy as an image for God's rule in the world was not always easy to appropriate in the biblical period. Ancient Israel's experience of monarchy was not positive. All but three of its kings were terrible disappointments. In Jesus' day, the family of Herod, whom most Jews rejected, sat on the throne—but only as clients of the hated Roman emperor. The importance of "the kingdom of heaven" for Matthew makes it impossible for us to ignore this image so central to his Gospel.

Defining Our Thematic Context

Yesterday we considered what Matthew has to say about Jesus. We reflected on the categories of Jewish religious thought that the evangelist reinterpreted to describe his experience of Jesus and to shape the beliefs of his fellow Christians about Jesus, the Messiah. Today we will reflect on Jesus' teaching about "the kingdom of heaven" and how Matthew reinterpreted Jewish hopes about the restoration of Jewish independence in the homeland of Palestine. While Matthew did reinterpret these expectations, he suggested a traditional path to their fulfillment: the law and the prophets.

Matthew was convinced that Christians ought to shape their lives of conversion by the values of traditional Jewish morality as found in the law and the prophets. He wants them to take the lead in the transformation of this world into a place where the sovereignty of God is manifest. Still, Matthew wants the Christian community to express its new life in Christ in traditional Jewish categories. He believes that the Jewish ethical system will be an effective guide to Christians as they hasten the day when "the kingdom of heaven" will be manifest in its fullness.

Opening Prayer

Blessed are you, Lord, king of the ages, who has given us your commandments. May we find in these commandments spirit and life, and may our keeping of your commandments transform this world of ours into a world of justice, peace and love. May it be a world in which you are sovereign and every evil power banished. We ask this through Christ our Lord. Amen.

RETREAT SESSION THREE

In the world of the Bible monarchy was more than pageantry. The ancient Egyptians thought of their king as the incarnation of a god. The obedience to the king's will insured the stability of their world. Disobedience led to disaster. The Semitic peoples of the East believed that their kings were the viceroys of their gods. The gods ruled through the kings they themselves set up. Two king lists from ancient Mesopotamia begin with the clause: "When kingship descended from the heavens...." The people of ancient Israel, too, thought of their kings as having been chosen by God. Speaking in God's name, the prophet Nathan assured David,

> Now therefore thus you shall say to my servant David: "Thus says the LORD of hosts: I took you from the pasture, from following the sheep to be prince over my people Israel." (2 Samuel 7:8)

This belief in the divine election of kings was necessary for ancient Israel since the Israelite tribes lived in their land for at least two hundred years without any kings to rule over them. The rituals of the Temple not only asserted that it was God who established the monarchy but also that the king was "God's son":

> "I have set my king on Zion, my holy hill."
> I will tell of the decree of the LORD:
> He said to me, "You are my son;
> today I have begotten you." (Psalm 2:6-7)

This inflated language used to speak of Israel's king made it very difficult to accept the fall of the Davidic dynasty, which took place almost six hundred years before Jesus was born. Jewish kings did rule over the territory of David's kingdom for about a hundred years following the Jewish victories in the Maccabean wars, but many Jews did not consider those kings legitimate since they were not of David's line. By Jesus' day, even that dynasty ended when Herod killed its last male members. During Jesus' ministry, the Roman emperor ruled Palestine though Herod's sons had authority over portions of the region as Roman client-rulers. When the Jews looked to the future, they envisioned the end of Roman rule and the restoration of the Davidic dynasty, remembering the promise that God made to David, "Your house and your kingdom shall be made sure forever before me; your throne shall be established forever" (2 Samuel 7:16).

Though a human being might sit on Israel's throne, some people recognized that this king presided over what was really God's kingdom. For example, the chronicler rendered God's promise to David a bit differently: "I [God] will confirm him [the king] in my house and in my kingdom forever, and his throne shall be established forever" (1 Chronicles 17:14).

The Chronicler speaks not of *David's* house and kingdom but of *God's* house and kingdom. The difference between the text in 2 Samuel and the later text in 1 Chronicles is significant. It underscores the notion that the role of the king in Israel is to ensure that people can recognize the rule of God in their lives. When it became clear that the Davidic dynasty was not going to be restored following its fall in the sixth century B.C., Jews began thinking about their future in terms of a divinely engineered restoration of Davidic rule. Still, it is clear that in the future that God has in store for Israel, it will be God who will be Israel's king. When Jesus taught his disciples how to pray, he instructed them to ask God to hasten the day of this divine rule over Israel and indeed over the whole world:

> Your kingdom come.
> Your will be done,
> on earth as it is in heaven." (Matthew 6:10)

Jesus, then, envisioned the future as most of his Jewish contemporaries did. Like them he waited for the day when God's sovereignty would manifest itself dramatically and unmistakably. That day would be a day of great happiness for all Israel. Jesus taught his disciples to make sense of their present circumstances by relating them to the coming of God's reign in this world. When God rules this world, all the powers of evil will be ineffectual. Roles will be reversed: The powers that currently control this world will themselves experience dispossession. The poor will become rich and the rich poor:

> [God] has brought down the powerful from their
>   thrones,
> and lifted up the lowly;
> [God] has filled the hungry with good things,
> and sent the rich away empty. (Luke 1:52-53)

In speaking of the future that God has in store for believers, Jesus used the term "kingdom." In the first three Gospels, "the kingdom of God" is the central motif of Jesus' preaching. Following Jewish custom, Matthew avoids using the name of God, so he uses the expression "the kingdom of heaven" instead of "the kingdom of God," which both Mark and Luke prefer. Jewish piety was so concerned to prevent the use of God's name "in vain" that it chose to use circumlocutions like "heaven" to refer to God. There is no real difference between Matthew's favored expression "the kingdom of heaven" and what Mark and Luke speak of as "the kingdom of God."

John the Baptist was the first to proclaim that "the kingdom of heaven" was near and Jesus took up the message from him. The words of both awakened in their contemporaries hopes that the long-expected restoration of the Davidic dynasty and Jewish political independence was about to take place. Believers were waiting in faith and hope for the manifestation of God's sovereignty over this world and they learned from both John and Jesus that their hopes were going to be fulfilled soon. Still, there were some differences in the way each proclaimed the coming of God's reign. John's preaching underscored divine judgment. God was coming to judge and purify Israel. The Baptist warned that no one could evade this coming judgment. John also pointed to someone who was to come after him: "His winnowing fork is in his hand, and he will clear his threshing floor and will gather his wheat into the granary; but the chaff he will burn with unquenchable fire" (3:12). The Baptist insisted that the people were to prepare for the coming of this judgment by repentance. They were to be baptized to show their readiness to repent.

When Jesus began his ministry, John wondered if he were "the one who is to come" (11:2). The Baptist had doubts because Jesus' proclamation differed from his own. First, while Jesus urged people to repent, he underscored the coming of the kingdom as God's saving power manifest in the world. Jesus then emphasized the priority of God's activity, which elicited the response of faith and repentance. Second, while Jesus did proclaim that the kingdom was about to come, he also asserted that the kingdom was already present. It was manifest in his person, in his preaching and in his healing. Jesus asserted that the great future proclaimed by the prophets and awaited by the pious had become present through him. He also claimed that people's response to his preaching will determine whether they will have a place in the kingdom of heaven when it is finally and fully revealed.

Matthew sees Jesus' miraculous power as proof that the kingdom of heaven has come. In particular, it is Jesus' power over demons that showed God has begun retaking this world from evil powers. When Jesus healed those whom Satan possessed, it was clear that the power of the Evil One was broken. When the Baptist sent some of his followers to ask, "Are you the one who is to come, or are we to wait for another?" (11:3), Jesus pointed to his miracles as proof that the kingdom of heaven had come through him:

> Go and tell John what you hear and see: the blind receive their sight, the lame walk, the lepers are cleansed, the deaf hear, the dead are raised, and the poor have good news brought to them. (11:4-5)

The kingdom of heaven, then, has already come through Jesus, whose miraculous power shows God's sovereignty over this world. Too many people understand miracles as suspension of the laws of nature that proves Jesus' divinity. Matthew understands the miracles as manifestations of the power of God who is exercising divine sovereignty through the ministry of Jesus. The disciples who carry on this ministry are also invested with miraculous power so that their proclamation of the kingdom might be credible as well.

While Jesus has shown God's sovereignty over this world, the kingdom has come only in a provisional manner. There is also a future dimension to the kingdom of heaven. That is the reason for Jesus' concluding his statement to John's followers by saying, "Blessed is anyone who takes no offense at me" (11:6).

The reason that some people may be disappointed in Jesus was precisely that the kingdom will be fully manifest only some time in the future. Jesus told his disciples several times that the kingdom was still hidden. This is the message of several parables: the sower, the weeds, the mustard seed, the yeast. Like the mustard seed, the kingdom must sprout and grow, though no one knows just how this is done. This tiny seed appears to have an inner power that propels it beyond all types of obstacles. The great obstacle in Jesus' life was the cross. It was Jesus' obedience that overcame even the power of death. The risen Jesus commissioned his disciples to proclaim the kingdom to all nations since it is not for Israel alone but is to embrace all peoples.

What is the relationship of the kingdom that Jesus proclaimed and the Church? There is, of course, an intimate connection between the two though they are not identical. The Church is the assembly of those who believe in Christ and continue his proclamation of the kingdom. Thus, the Church is an organ of the kingdom which is the totality of Christ's saving presence in the world.

The Church's mission is to hasten the day of the final and complete revelation of divine sovereignty by proclaiming the gospel to all nations in obedience to the command of Christ. The Church is also the first-fruits of the kingdom of heaven. It is to be a sign of what is yet to come. Its inclusion of all people in the community of faith should foster reconciliation. Its commitment to the ideals of the gospel ought to be a prelude to a new sense of morality in the world. Its willingness to walk the way of the cross with Christ points to the renunciation that people need to make in order to be of service to each other.

The identification of the Church with the kingdom of heaven characteristic of the Middle Ages led the reformers to speak of the kingdom in a spiritual and individualistic sense: It is God's grace and spirit in the hearts of people. The reformers ignored the positive significance that the kingdom was to have on life in this world. But it is a mistake to so spiritualize the kingdom that there is no possibility of its penetrating the present world. The kingdom of heaven is one way to speak about God's activity in this world. The believer is to live so as to make visible that divine presence. The Church, then, is the community of those who commit themselves to bringing Christ's message of the kingdom to the world. It cannot be simply a spiritual reality. The reality of the kingdom comes from its penetration into this world.

The future dimension of the kingdom does not mean that we are to ignore its present reality. Hope for the final and decisive manifestation of divine sovereignty over this world does not mean that we ignore the present. Our belief in the future triumph of the kingdom makes it possible for us to give ourselves completely to the service of the kingdom. This is clear from the beatitudes (5:3-12). Jesus commends behaviors that make no sense in view of this age while asserting that the poor, the sorrowful and persecuted will inherit the kingdom in the future. We know, then, that our sacrifices for the sake of the kingdom will not be made in vain. When Jesus returns in power, he will join our feeble efforts to his own and then present a renewed world to God—a world that submits to the sovereignty of God. It is only when Jesus returns that the kingdom of heaven will be completely manifest.

The question we have to face is what we are to do in the meantime. Does the inevitable triumph of the kingdom mean that we can wait passively for that triumph? In Jesus' ministry, the future dimensions of the kingdom shaped his ministry in the present. Similarly, the future that we believe in must shape our present. The moral choices we make, the way we live in this world, the values we have—all these flow from our faith and hope in the kingdom that will be fully revealed only in the future. Thus, our future determines our present.

The people of Jesus' day were acutely aware of the socioeconomic predicament of their lives. They did not control their own political or economic destiny. They were subject to the Roman emperor and their homeland was occupied by foreign legions to enforce Roman rule. The Romans even renamed the territory of the former Israelite kingdoms "Palestine" after the Philistines, the great antagonists of the Israelite tribes. While Galilee, the region where Jesus grew up, was ruled by a member of Herod's family, that ruler held power only as a Roman client. Judea and Jerusalem were ruled directly by a Roman procurator. During Jesus' ministry, the procurator was Pontius Pilate. The effect of these political circumstances served to intensify the hopes for the in-breaking of the kingdom of heaven. Though Jesus' notion of the kingdom of heaven did not include the restoration of Jewish rule over Palestine, the Romans took no chances and had Jesus executed once they heard that people called him "king of the Jews." They found him guilty of political insurrection and Pilate intended a cruel irony with the charge he placed on Jesus' cross: "This is Jesus, the King of the Jews" (27:37).

The acute problems that Jesus' fellow Jews faced in Palestine did not dispose them to focus on the future dimension of the kingdom of heaven that Jesus proclaimed. They wanted the kingdom to come immediately to effect a restoration of Jewish fortunes in Palestine. The comfortable life-style of most of us today leads to a different problem. We fail to see the present dimension of the kingdom that Jesus proclaimed. We think of the kingdom as something that belongs to the far-off future. Doing so, however, leads to the abandonment of the present to the powers of evil. While the fullness of the kingdom is a future reality, we should not fail the present. Our belief in the final triumph of divine sovereignty ought to shape our present.

Another problem that contemporary believers face is their tendency to spiritualize the kingdom of heaven. This particularly affects Americans whose political tradition keeps religious belief on the margins of public life. In such a setting, religion becomes a deeply personal and interior matter. While religious belief is deeply personal, it calls for an external expression. Faith ought to lead to practice. Belief ought to dictate life-style. Commitment to God ought to lead to a commitment to neighbor:

> When the Pharisees heard that he had silenced the Sadducees, they gathered together, and one of them, a lawyer, asked him a question to test him. "Teacher, which commandment in the law is the greatest?" He said to him, "'You shall love the Lord your God with all your heart, and with all your soul, and with all your mind.' This is the greatest and first commandment. And a second is like it: 'You shall love your neighbor as yourself.' On these two commandments hang all the law and the prophets." (22:34-40)

Of course, the love that Jesus was speaking of did not confine itself to feelings alone. For Jesus, love was an activity that proved itself through obedience to God and service to neighbor. Christianity, as Matthew envisioned it, was to be shaped by the law and the prophets, whose message Jesus summarized as love of God and love of neighbor. The law, then, provides a framework within which believers give shape to their lives of conversion. The effects of their conversion are not confined to their interior lives. Conversion manifests itself in efforts to lead all people to experience the effects of God's sovereignty over this world.

An authentic notion of the kingdom of heaven stresses the visible and communal significance of the kingdom. The Second Vatican Council recognized this. The bishops produced not only a Dogmatic Constitution on the Church but a pastoral one on the Church in the Modern World. When composition of this second document was suggested, there was some objection from those who believed that the Church was to set the agenda for the world, whose responsibility, in turn, is to hear and accept the Church's spiritual teaching. Suggesting that the Church respond to the social, political and economic needs of people implied that the world was setting the agenda for the Church. When the Second Vatican Council approved the Pastoral Constitution on the "Church in the Modern World" ("*Gaudium et Spes*"), it reminded Christians of Jesus' words that they were to be salt for the earth and light for the world.

Matthew's metaphor "salt for the earth" is particularly apt when applied to the role of Christians in the world. Usually we think of salt either as a flavor enhancement or as a preservative. Matthew's metaphor has neither of these uses in mind, but another that also was common in the Palestine of his day. The ordinary fuel for cooking was dried animal dung. Other fuels were too rare and expensive. But dried dung was not the most efficient of fuels. It needed a catalyst to enhance its combustibility. Salt was this catalyst. Rock salt was kneaded into moist dung, which was then set in the sun for drying. After the dried dung was consumed in the oven, the salt remained and was reclaimed to be used again. Eventually the old salt lost its catalytic qualities and had to be discarded in favor of a new supply. Jesus then was calling his disciples to serve as catalysts for good in the world. If they do not, they will be cast aside like so much old salt. This may not be the most agreeable metaphor, but it gets the job done.

Matthew had very definite ideas on what the authentic disciple ought to do to hasten the day of the Lord's return and the final revelation of God's sovereignty. He believed that the law and the prophets provide the followers of Jesus a pattern for the transformation of the world. The revelation that God gave to ancient Israel continued to offer the disciples guidance as they tried to live out their commitment to God and neighbor. Matthew was convinced that the Scriptures (the Old Testament) can continue to serve the original purpose of giving shape to the believer's life with God. The Scriptures lost none of their validity or relevance: "Not one letter, not one stroke of a letter will pass from the law until all is accomplished" (5:18).

While Paul, a Jew from the Diaspora, introduced some insights from Greco-Roman moral philosophy into Christian ethics, Matthew was certain that the Hebrew ethical tradition offers the Church all that is needed to fulfill the divine will. The evangelist is dismayed with some of his fellow Christians who are ready to leave behind the Jewish moral tradition, so he asserts the continuing importance the Torah has for the Christian community:

> ...[W]hoever breaks one of the least of these
> commandments and teaches others to do the same,
> will be called least in the kingdom of heaven; but
> whoever does them and teaches these
> commandments will be called great in the kingdom
> of heaven. (Matthew 5:19)

While Matthew has some disagreements with his fellow
Christians about the significance of the law, he has more
serious conflicts with the Pharisaic pattern of observance.
He implies that mimimalism is a principle characteristic
of Pharisaism and maintains that Christian observance
must be qualitatively different from that of the Pharisees:

> For I tell you, unless your righteousness exceeds
> that of the scribes and Pharisees, you will never
> enter the kingdom of heaven. (5:20)

To underscore the need for Christians to engage
themselves in the transformation of the world, Matthew
tells them that faith without good deeds is not enough for
those who would enter the kingdom of heaven:

> Not everyone who says to me, 'Lord, Lord,' will
> enter the kingdom of heaven, but only the one who
> does the will of my Father in heaven. (7:21)

For the evangelist, then, the Christian life involved
engagement in the world. It meant feeding the hungry,
giving drink to the thirsty, clothing the naked, welcoming
the stranger, visiting the sick and the imprisoned. No
religious achievements are sufficient substitutions for
meeting the needs of others. Even those who prophesy,
exorcise demons or perform miracles in the name of
Christ cannot rely on those achievements alone to sustain
them on the day of judgment. Jesus expects nothing less
than the transformation of the world.

While engagement in the world is important, while
acts of righteousness that surpass those of the scribes and

Pharisees are necessary and while living according to the law and the prophets are essential, Matthew wants to make it clear that the disciples are not to look for recognition. He compares the greatest in the kingdom of heaven with a child:

> At that time the disciples came to Jesus and asked, "Who is the greatest in the kingdom of heaven?" He called a child, whom he put among them, and said, "Truly I tell you, unless you change and become like children, you will never enter the kingdom of heaven. Whoever becomes humble like this child is the greatest in the kingdom of heaven." (18:1-4)

Our relationship with God, then, is never our achievement, as if we earned it by our righteousness. Like children, who are completely dependent upon the love of their parents, so we are completely dependent upon God's love. Our good deeds do not place God in our debt as if God owed us something because of our obedience. Our relationship with God always remains an act of God's grace that we can never earn, but can only receive with gratitude.

Matthew illustrates the grace of God and the consequences it ought to have in our lives with the parable of the unforgiving debtor:

> [T]he kingdom of heaven may be compared to a king who wished to settle accounts with his slaves. When he began the reckoning, one who owed him ten thousand talents was brought to him; and as he could not pay, his lord ordered him to be sold, together with his wife and children and all his possessions, and payment to be made. So the slave fell on his knees before him, saying, 'Have patience with me, and I will pay you everything.' And out of pity for him, the lord of that slave released him and forgave him the debt. But that same slave, as he

went out, came upon one of his fellow slaves who
owed him a hundred denarii; and seizing him by the
throat, he said, 'Pay what you owe.' Then his fellow
slave fell down and pleaded with him, 'Have
patience with me, and I will pay you.' But he
refused; then he went and threw him into prison
until he would pay the debt. When his fellow slaves
saw what had happened, they were greatly
distressed, and they went and reported to their lord
all that had taken place. Then his lord summoned
him and said to him, 'You wicked slave! I forgave
you all that debt because you pleaded with me.
Should you not have had mercy on your fellow
slave, as I had mercy on you?' And in anger his lord
handed him over to be tortured until he would pay
his entire debt. So my heavenly Father will also do
to every one of you, if you do not forgive your
brother or sister from your heart. (18:23-35)

The experience of God's graciousness is to lead us to offer
forgiveness to all. Life with God is not like a commercial
transaction. It is not based on reciprocity; rather God
gives and we receive. The forgiveness we extend to others
is not based on their worthiness but our need to do for
others what God has done for us. Matthew was acutely
aware of how easy it is to misunderstand the dynamics of
a life with God based on the Torah. A surface reading of
the Book of Deuteronomy leads one to conclude that
obedience brings blessing and disobedience brings a
curse—as simple as that. Books like Job and Ecclesiastes,
however, make it clear that life with God is not such a
simple matter. These books complement the Torah by
showing that, while obedience is necessary, there are no
guarantees in this world—a world still under the control
of the powers of evil. That is why we wait in hope for the
revelation of God's sovereignty over this world. While we
wait, we are obedient in response to the grace of God

given us in Jesus Christ. While we wait, we extend the forgiveness we have received to all without exception.

Another parable that Matthew uses to underscore the graciousness of God is the parable of the laborers in the vineyard:

"[T]he kingdom of heaven is like a landowner who went out early in the morning to hire laborers for his vineyard. After agreeing with the laborers for the usual daily wage, he sent them into his vineyard. When he went out about nine o'clock, he saw others standing idle in the marketplace; and he said to them, 'You also go into the vineyard, and I will pay you whatever is right.' So they went. When he went out again about noon, and about three o'clock, he did the same. And about five o'clock, he went out and found others standing around; and he said to them, 'Why are you standing here idle all day?' They said to him, 'Because no one has hired us.' He said to them, 'You too also into the vineyard.' When evening came, the owner of the vineyard said to his managers, 'Call the laborers and give them their pay, beginning with the last and then going to the first.' When those hired about five o'clock came, each of them received the usual daily wage. Now when the first came, they thought they would receive more, but each of them also received the usual wage. And when they received it, they grumbled against the landowner, saying, 'These last worked only one hour, and you have made them equal to us who have borne the burden of the day and the scorching heat.' But he replied to one of them, 'Friend, I am doing you no wrong; did you not agree with me for the usual daily wage? Take what belongs to you and go; I choose to give to this last the same as I give to you. Am I not allowed to do what I choose with what belongs to me? Or are you envious because I am generous?' So the last will be first, and the first will be last." (20:1-16)

Like most of Jesus' parables, this one challenged the cultural and religious assumptions of those who heard it. Naturally their sympathies were with those who protested the landowner's pay scale. When the last hired received a denarius, a laborer's daily wage, those who worked all day assumed that they were going to receive a proportionately higher amount since they worked more. Those who were listening to Jesus tell his story expected him to conclude his tale by describing the reward of those who worked the full day. They could only imagine what it might be since those who worked only a single hour received payment for a full day. Jesus, however, surprised them by having all the workers receive the same wage without regard for the time they labored. Matthew included this parable in his Gospel because he did not want his readers to approach the law and the prophets with the notion that they were meeting their obligations.

Matthew believed that the Jewish ethical tradition had much more to offer than a list of obligations. He also believed that the Christians ought to shape their lives according to this moral tradition without, however, lapsing into minimalism and obligationism.

Matthew was convinced that the law offered Christians the way to hasten the coming of the kingdom of heaven. He could only imagine the effect of people observing the law—not out of a sense of obligation and burden—but out of a sense of gratitude to God for the salvation they have received in Jesus Christ. This gratitude would engender a generosity of spirit such that the law's full potential for creating a new world would become obvious. Freed from the burden of mere obligations, Christians would be limited only by their gratitude, generosity, and creativity in expressing their love of God through their love of neighbor.

Matthew leads us away from an appropriation of the

kingdom of heaven that merely spiritualizes this central feature of Jesus' teaching. The kingdom of heaven is about real people, living in this time, facing serious economic, political and social crises. Matthew is convinced that the moral values in the Hebrew Bible will help Christians respond to our brothers and sisters in need. Our faith in Jesus' victory over the powers of evil enables us to deal with these issues without fearing that our efforts will be in vain. The real battle against the powers of evil has been fought and won. What remains for us is to hasten the day when everyone will experience the full extent of Christ's victory. We believe that when Jesus returns to claim his throne, he will join our feeble efforts to his own and then present a renewed world to God. That will be the beginning of the kingdom of heaven in its fullness.

Through our living the ideals of the gospel we show to the world what life under the sovereignty of God can be like. Jesus, who has called us to his kingdom, also calls us to lead lives worthy of the gospel. He calls us to be light of the world and salt of the earth. Jesus calls us to nothing less than the transformation of our world.

For Reflection

- *What is the Lord asking you to do in order to hasten the coming of the kingdom of heaven in its fullness?*

- *What is the greatest obstacle in your life preventing you from committing yourself to the proclamation of the kingdom of heaven?*

- *How have you already experienced Christ's victory over the powers of evil? What is the place of the law and the prophets in your life with God?*

Closing Prayer

Our Father, who art in heaven,
hallowed be Thy Name,
Thy kingdom come,
Thy will be done on earth as it is in heaven.
Give us this day our daily bread.
Forgive us our trespasses
as we forgive those who trespass against us.
Lead us not into temptation,
but deliver us from evil. Amen.

DAY FOUR
Raising Up Disciples

Coming Together in the Spirit

A passage from the Mishnah[1]—a collection of Pharisaic and rabbinic legal traditions compiled by Judah the Prince about two hundred years after Christ—shows the importance that Jewish religious teachers gave to discipleship.

> Moses received the Law from Sinai and committed it to Joshua, and Joshua to the elders, and the elders to the Prophets, and the Prophets committed it to the men of the Great Synagogue. They said three things: Be deliberate in judgment, raise up many disciples, and make a fence around the Law. (*Pirke Avot* 1:1)

Every Jewish male was to seek out a teacher so that he could learn the law and the traditions of the elders, which was God's revelation to Israel. The teacher is the living link to the "men of the Great Synagogue" and through them to Moses and ultimately Sinai which is, of course, a pious way of referring to God.

Even gentiles were attracted by the energy and care which religious Jews dedicated to the study of their law and the traditional interpretations and applications of that law to daily life. To an outsider, however, sometimes this study appears to concern itself with minutiae that are hardly relevant to most people. A cynical gentile once gave this challenge to a leading rabbi: "I will convert if you can teach me the whole law while standing on one foot." The rabbi accepted the challenge and lifted one foot off the ground while saying, "Love your neighbor as yourself. This is the Law. The rest is commentary."

Today we will look at Jesus as a teacher who calls us to be his students. To those who answer his call, Jesus becomes more than a conduit leading back to Moses. Jesus is their Messiah, the "one who is to come," the son of David who points the way to the kingdom of heaven. Jesus was no ordinary teacher—all agreed on that (see Matthew 7:29). Being a disciple of his was an experience like no other. What can we, today's disciples, learn from Matthew about discipleship?

Defining Our Thematic Context

The kingdom of heaven will not come with one swift, divine stroke. It will come because of what Jesus did and what his followers will do. The miracles of Jesus show that the kingdom has come through his ministry, but Jesus sent out his disciples after giving them "authority over unclean spirits, to cast them out, and to cure every disease and every sickness" (10:1). Jesus' blood shed on the cross nourished the beginnings of the kingdom of heaven and he tells those who would follow him: Those who "want to become my followers, let them deny themselves and take up their cross..." (16:24).

What Matthew has to say about discipleship flows directly from what he has to say about the kingdom of heaven. If the kingdom of heaven means that Christians are to engage the world and transform it, discipleship sets before us the principles for that engagement and the means of that transformation. Today we listen to what Jesus has to say to his first disciples. All that he said to them, he says to us.

Opening Prayer

Lord Jesus, we thank you for calling us to be your disciples. Give us a generous spirit as we answer that call. Help us to overcome our human weakness as we try to carry out the divine mandate that you have given us. You have blessed us with your gifts. May we use them in the service of our sisters and brothers in need. Let us be for them "salt" and "light." Make us catalysts for good, instruments of your peace and promoters of your justice so that people can see the good we do and give you the glory. Be with us now, as you promised, so that we can fulfill your commission to make disciples of all nations. Amen.

RETREAT SESSION FOUR

Matthew's portrait of Jesus depicts him in colors typical of early Judaism. The evangelist describes Jesus as a teacher with a group of disciples around him. For example, he begins the story of the Sermon on the Mount by setting the scene. "When Jesus saw the crowds, he went up the mountain; and after he sat down, his disciples came to him. Then he began to speak, and taught them, saying..." (5:1-2).

A similar introduction could be used to set the scene for describing almost any other Jewish teacher instructing his disciples. Matthew does speak of the Pharisees' disciples, students of those who encouraged the practice of the oral law—which Jesus rejected. Matthew explicitly contrasts Jesus, the teacher, with other Jewish teachers. He points out that Jesus' teaching made a deep impression on the people because he taught them with authority, unlike their own scribes.

Jesus' contemporaries regarded him as a teacher, though it was common knowledge that Jesus had none of the training that prepared someone to be a religious teacher. Still, Jesus accepted this designation and spoke of himself as "the teacher." There were some significant differences between Jesus and other Jewish teachers. First, Jesus calls his disciples to follow and learn from him. This differs from the normal practice among other Jews. It was usually the duty of the student to find a teacher who would accept him. The prospective students often had to prove that they were capable and therefore worthy to be included among their teacher's students. On the contrary, the story of the call of Matthew implies that Jesus called some who lacked the necessary moral qualifications, since he even included a tax collector among his disciples.

Second, only men were permitted to become students. Respected teachers were not even to be seen in public with women—including their wives. Matthew notes that at the cross "[m]any women were also there, looking on from a distance; they had followed Jesus from Galilee..." (27:55). Though Matthew does not call these women "disciples," he clearly states that they accompanied Jesus just as his male disciples. Unlike them, however, the women did not abandon Jesus in his final hours. Finally, the dominant element in the teacher/student relationship in early Judaism was the Torah. It was not the teacher's authority that was final; it was that of the Torah. The teacher was merely a conduit handing on the tradition of

Moses that he had received. In Matthew, however, the disciples' first commitment is to the person of Jesus and this commitment has precedence over all others. "Another man, one of the disciples, said to (Jesus), 'Lord, let me go and bury my father first.' But Jesus said, 'Follow me, and let the dead bury their own dead'" (8:21-22).

Who were Jesus' disciples? They were a diverse lot. Among the Twelve there was a zealot, several fishermen, a tax collector, a Judean, several Galileans. Some, like Philip and Andrew, had Greek names; others had Semitic names. How diverse the wider group of Jesus' followers was we can only guess. Included in this wider circle were women and "a rich man of Arimathea" among others. The selection of such a group showed that Jesus was sensitive to the diversity of the Judaism of his day. For Jews like the zealots, it was important that they rid their homeland of the Romans and restore an independent Jewish state ruled by a Jewish king. Other Jews, like tax collectors, collaborated with the Roman occupiers. For some Jews, it was important to consciously integrate the values of Greek culture that were compatible with their ancestral religious traditions into Judaism. For others, it was necessary to keep separate from any foreign ideas no matter how attractive. Some Jews were insistent on careful observance of the Torah. Others whose occupations made strict observance impossible had to find other ways to remain faithful to their religious traditions. A minority of Jews tried to live according to Pharisaic teaching; most—especially the Jews of Galilee— did not. There was no one way of being a Jew in Jesus' day and his choice of disciples reflected that pluralism. It is little wonder, then, that the disciples quarreled among themselves. There were serious differences among them and these were bound to surface occasionally.

In calling his disciples Jesus chose not to avoid the

inherent tensions that come with selecting a diverse group, because along with those inevitable tensions come possibilities that a homogeneous group could not offer. We sometimes think pluralism and diversity are twentieth-century phenomena. Of course they are not. Jesus had to take these into account as he called those who were to be his disciples. That he chose as diverse a group as he did shows that he had a realistic understanding of the social and religious dynamics of his society, and that he sought to meet people where they were.

Thus, we need to be ready to accept the differences among the disciples of Jesus today. What is the one thing that Mother Angelica, Theresa Kane, Charles Curran, Cardinal Law, Ralph Martin, Daniel Berrigan, Rosemary Ruether, William F. Buckley, Ted Kennedy, Joseph Scheidler have in common? All are Catholics—though they express their religious commitments in very different ways. The diversity among Jesus' followers has always been great. Think of Francis and Dominic, Teresa of Avila and Therese of Lisieux, Mary and Martha, Aquinas and Scotus, Pius IX and John XXIII, Augustine and Jerome, Margaret of Cortona and Maria Goretti, Mother Cabrini and Bernadette Soubirous and Ignatius of Loyola and Don Bosco. Imagine all the gifts that the Church and the world would not have received if all the disciples of Jesus were cut from the same cloth.

The key to benefiting from the diversity among Jesus' followers is an unwillingness to make absolute one pattern for the following of Christ. Just think of the great contributions the various religious orders have made to Christian spirituality. There is Benedictine spirituality, Franciscan spirituality, Carmelite spirituality, Jesuit spirituality, Dominican spirituality. These different approaches continue to nourish the lives of so many religious and lay people that it is difficult to imagine the

Church without any one of these. The different "schools" of the spiritual life can flourish only in an atmosphere that not only respects but encourages diversity among the disciples of Jesus today.

Unfortunately, today there is less tolerance for pluralism among Jesus' followers than there needs to be. Conservatives and liberals in the Church find themselves standing further and further apart. Liberals need to recognize that the conservative position is a legitimate one. Conservatives need to remember that the liberals love the Church as much as they do. Both need to avoid making absolute their respective positions. Since we are human and incapable of comprehending the mystery that is God, we can each have only partial insights into that mystery. It does not make much sense to consider our partial insights as absolute. It makes even less sense to impose our way of thinking on others.

Next, what does Jesus expect of those whom he calls to be his disciples? For Matthew, the principal obligation of the disciple is to obey Jesus. Following Jesus begins with a decision to leave all else behind.

> Whoever loves father or mother more than me is not worthy of me; and whoever loves son or daughter more than me is not worthy of me; and whoever does not take up the cross and follow me is not worthy of me. (10:37-38)

Once the disciples make this commitment to follow Jesus, they obey him as servants obey their masters. Their obedience should reflect diligence and vigilance.

> Who, then, is the faithful and wise slave, whom his master has put in charge of his household to give the other slaves their allowance of food at the proper time? Blessed is that slave whom his master will find at work when he arrives. Truly I tell you,

> he will put that one in charge of all his possessions.
> But if that wicked slave says to himself, 'My master
> is delayed,' and he begins to beat his fellow slaves,
> and eats and drinks with drunkards, the master of
> that slave will come on a day when he does not
> expect him and at an hour that he does not know.
> He will cut him in pieces and put him with the
> hypocrites, where there will be weeping and
> gnashing of teeth. (24:45-51)

Jesus' disciples listen to his teaching not simply to
appropriate his words intellectually but to be formed by
them for obedience. Still, the disciples are more than mere
students of Jesus, learning his teaching to prepare
themselves to carry on his ministry. The disciples become
Jesus' true family:

> While he was still speaking to the crowds, his
> mother and his brothers appeared outside, wishing
> to speak with him. [Someone told him, "Your
> mother and your brothers are standing outside,
> asking to speak with you."] But he said in reply to
> the one who told him, "Who is my mother? Who are
> my brothers?" And stretching out his hand toward
> his disciples, he said, "Here are my mother and my
> brothers.
> For whoever does the will of my Father in heaven
> is my brother and sister and mother." (12:46-50)

Jesus demands that his disciples renounce all—including
their families—to follow him. If they do, they become
part of a new family committed solely to fulfilling the will
of the One who sent Jesus into the world to bring the
Good News.

The disciples of the rabbis will themselves become
rabbis one day, but the disciples of Jesus will always
remain disciples. Their lives will always be shaped by his
words. While he charges them to carry out the ministry of

the gospel, it is always his teaching that they convey. They heal the sick in his name. They are persecuted because they are his followers. Still, they enjoy the care of the God who commissioned Jesus. Finally their witness to him before people in this age will result in Jesus' speaking for them in the age to come.

A unique aspect of following Jesus involves the disciples' being sent on the way of the cross. The disciples' fellowship with Jesus means that they will be drawn into the mystery of his passion and death:

> Beware of them, for they will hand you over to councils and flog you in their synagogues; and you will be dragged before governors and kings because of me.... Brother will betray brother to death, and a father his child, and children will rise against parents and have them put to death; and you will be hated by all because of my name. But the one who endures to the end will be saved. (10:17-18, 21-22)

The disciples of Jesus will share their master's fate, but they will also share his vindication if they remain faithful.

These are the ideals of discipleship: commitment to the person of Jesus, renunciation for the sake of the gospel, participation in Jesus' mission of teaching and healing, sharing in suffering and experiencing his vindication. What are the realities of discipleship? How did the real people who answered Jesus' call to follow him live out their commitment? Let's look at Jesus' first disciples. While they immediately and eagerly answered Jesus' call, they failed to understand him, his mission and his message. That is quite an indictment, but that is precisely the image that Matthew gives of the disciples. They had their fears:

> A windstorm arose on the sea, so great that the boat was being swamped by the waves; but he was asleep. And they went and woke him up saying,

"Lord, save us! We are perishing!" And he said to them, "Why are you afraid, you of little faith?" Then he got up and rebuked the winds and the sea; and there was a dead calm. They were amazed, saying "What sort of man is this, that even the winds and the sea obey him?" (8:23-27)

When danger threatened, the disciples' fearfulness got the better of them. Jesus asked them about the quality of their faith. After the danger passed through the power of Jesus, the disciples were left asking each other what sort of man was their teacher.

The disciples had their quarrels:
Then the mother of the sons of Zebedee came to [Jesus] with her sons, and kneeling before him, she asked a favor of him. He said to her, "What do you want?" She said to him, "Declare that these two sons of mine will sit, one at your right hand, and one at your left, in your kingdom...." When the ten heard it, they were angry with the two brothers. But Jesus called them to him and said, "You know that the rulers of the Gentiles lord it over them, and the great ones are tyrants over them. It will not be so among you; but whoever wishes to be great among you must be your servant, and whoever wishes to be first among you must be your slave; just as the Son of Man came not to be served but to serve, and to give his life as a ransom for many." (20:20-21, 24-28)

Jesus came to serve, but his disciples thought of their own position, authority, and power in the kingdom of heaven. They believed that Jesus came to restore the political and economic fortunes of the Jewish people. They would again enjoy political independence and economic prosperity. As Jesus' associates, the disciples thought that they would enjoy prominent positions in the new Jewish state. Their precise standing in the kingdom that Jesus was going to establish was the subject of their quarrels. Jesus used these as an occasion to show the disciples that leadership meant service. Of course, they were to play critically important roles in the community of believers, but these roles were of service—not domination.

The disciples objected when Jesus spoke about his destiny—about the rejection, trial and death that awaited him in Jerusalem. Matthew has Jesus speak about his coming passion on three different occasions: after Peter's confession, after the Transfiguration, and on the way to Jerusalem. After the first prediction, Peter is most adamant in protests. Matthew simply notes that after the second prediction, "a great sadness came over (the disciples)." It appears by the third prediction, the disciples had become accustomed to Jesus' words about his fate and chose to simply ignore them and began arguing about their future roles in the kingdom. When the disciples were confronted with the reality of Jesus' predictions in the Garden of Gethsemane, Matthew records their reaction without elaboration. "Then all the disciples deserted him and fled" (26:56). After following Jesus through the villages of Galilee, hearing his words and seeing his mighty deeds, it has come to this: a flight in the night that left Jesus to face his fate alone—without those whom he called his mother and his brothers.

Why did Matthew paint such an unflattering portrait of Jesus' disciples? He was writing for our benefit—for those whom Jesus has called to be his disciples in this day. Jesus has called us to abandon ourselves to him, to commit all of our talents and energy to the proclamation of the kingdom. He asks us to renounce that which stands in the way of our fulfilling our mission. He reminds us that we, too, will have to take up our cross to follow him. But like Jesus' first disciples we will fail. At times, our fears will paralyze us. We will argue among ourselves as we try to dominate rather than to serve. We will not want to walk with Jesus in Jerusalem because it means being with him as he is rejected and condemned. We may even flee to "save" ourselves. What Matthew helps us to see is our dark side. We may have been excited about the gospel, but experience has shown us what following Christ entails and we are afraid, we protest, we flee. Still, what Matthew helps us to see is that our failures do not disqualify us from discipleship. Like the Eleven, rehabilitated by the risen Jesus, we, too, are commissioned to make disciples of all nations. Matthew helps us to have a realistic picture of ourselves as disciples.

This is the scandal of the Incarnation. God chose to be reconciled to us through the means of human flesh and blood. The humanity of Jesus—his flesh and blood—made it possible for people like the disciples to experience God touching their lives. At the same time, the humanity of Jesus made it difficult for others to accept Jesus for who he really was. During his trial before the Sanhedrin, Jesus acknowledged that he was the messiah, the Son of God. But the high priest, who led the interrogation could not see beyond the human being who was on trial before him. "He has blasphemed. Why do we still need witnesses?" (26:63) was Caiaphas' response to Jesus' confession.

Matthew begins his instruction for the disciples of Jesus today by reminding us that the greatest in the kingdom is like the child who depends upon its parents not on its own resources (18:1-4). Disciples of Jesus recognize their dependence on God's grace to remain committed to the gospel. Just as there is no student without a teacher, so there is no disciple without Jesus. Discipleship has as its foundation a loving, personal relationship with Jesus Christ. This relationship makes it possible for us to use our talents for the sake of the kingdom in an authentic fashion. Our only goal will be to serve our master in loving obedience without any hidden agenda of self-promotion or self-righteousness.

Next Matthew offers a stern warning against any disciple becoming a stumbling block for another (18:5-10). We should support each other in doing good, in being of service, in living lives worthy of the gospel. We should not lead each other into sin, in effect becoming Satans to each other. Jesus uses the most graphic language possible in speaking about this matter. He asserts that drowning in the sea is a better fate than that which awaits those who lead other disciples into sin. The evangelist immediately balances this harshness of Jesus' warnings with a saying about the lost sheep. Jesus assures us that he will go to the greatest lengths possible to return to the community of believers those who have fallen.

The evangelist follows this touching saying on forgiveness with some practical advice on dealing with the problems that will inevitably arise among the disciples. He suggests that the community not ignore the problem but deal with it in a straightforward fashion. Jesus tells his disciples that they need to speak with each other in love about their mutual failures:

> If another member of the church sins against you, go and point out the fault when the two of you are alone. If the member listens to you, you have regained that one. But if you are not listened to, take one or two others along with you, so that every word may be confirmed by the evidence of two or three witnesses. If the member refuses to listen to them, tell it to the church; and if the offender refuses to listen even to the church, let such a one be to you as a Gentile and a tax collector. (18:15-17)

Reconciliation is always to be preferred to breaking off the relationship of love that should exist between disciples. Only as a last and desperate resort should the disciples go their separate ways. We need to hear this message with special urgency. We cannot allow the differences among disciples to lead to hardening of contrary positions that make genuine reconciliation more difficult as each day passes. As Jesus instructs us, we need to listen to one another. Listening is the first step on the path that leads to reconciliation.

Matthew closes his chapter on the life of the disciples together by speaking about prayer and forgiveness (18:19-22). There is no better way to overcome divisions in the Church than for the disciples of Jesus to pray together. Jesus promises to be with the disciples when they pray (v. 20) and the presence of Jesus in their midst will help overcome the tensions, quarrels and fears that come when human beings are searching for God together. That we should expect our humanity to become an obstacle in our life with God is clear from Jesus' advice to Peter that he should be prepared to forgive those who wrong him "seventy times seven times" (18:22).

Concluding his teaching about the disciples' life together, Matthew cites Jesus' parable of the unforgiving debtor. This story reminds us that each of us without exception has been forgiven a debt that we could never hope to pay. If God has forgiven us, we then ought to forgive each other. The parable ends with a stern warning to those disciples who chose not to take the way of forgiveness. What they can expect from God is what they offer to their brothers and sisters: no mercy.

One constant in Matthew's Gospel is a call to join Jesus in fulfilling the mission given him by God. This is evident from the sayings of Jesus cited by Matthew, in several of Jesus' parables (such as the parable of the talents) and in the mission of the Twelve. The Twelve are to do Jesus' work on his authority. One principle guiding the ministry of the disciple is, "You received without payment; give without payment" (10:8b).

Every disciple is a beneficiary of God's grace without earning or meriting it. It follows then that every disciple ought to become an instrument that God can use for the salvation of others or—as Matthew has Jesus say—the disciples are to be "salt of the earth" and "light of the world." People ought to see the witness of the disciples and "give glory to God who is in heaven." The disciples are to use the talents they have received from God for the sake of bringing in as many as possible into the kingdom of heaven.

Mission, then, is not the calling of a special few. When Jesus called us to be his disciples, he called us to mission. We should not, however, understand this call in a narrow sense of leading people to the Catholic Church. Jesus calls us to serve the kingdom of heaven which is more comprehensive than the Church. Mission involves evangelization and the transformation of the social, political and economic order. It means taking people where they are and meeting their immediate needs—one of which is their need to respond with repentance to the proclamation of the gospel.

We need also to carefully discern what other needs people may have. For the homeless, it may be a hot meal and a warm and safe place to spend the night. For the young people, it may be a sympathetic ear to appreciate the tremendous and difficult changes they are going through. For people in the world of business, it may be help with integrating their work with the ideals of the gospel. For the single parent, it may be help with caring for their children. For the elderly, it may be a visit that relieves their loneliness. For the refugee, it may be help with securing legal status. For the physically challenged, it may be making places of worship accessible.

Through the death and Resurrection of Jesus and the ministry of the Church, we have the experience of being reconciled with God. We want to share that experience with all our brothers and sisters for what we have freely received we will freely give. The only limits there will be on our effectiveness in mission are the level of our generosity, the creativity of our response to the gospel and our sensitivity to the needs of others. What Jesus teaches us through Matthew's Gospel is that our life with God cannot remain on a personal and individual plane. Even a cloistered contemplative like Thomas Merton became involved in the civil rights movement because he realized that the gospel does not offer us the luxury of an uninvolved Christian life.

> All authority in heaven and on earth has been given to me. Go therefore, and make disciples of all nations, baptizing them in the name of the Father and of the Son and of the Holy Spirit, and teaching them to obey all that I have commanded you. (28:18b-20a)

Like other Jewish religious teachers, Jesus raised up disciples. They were a diverse lot. They were not perfect. But they learned from him what it means to obey the will of God. And from Jesus, they received the commission to "make disciples of all nations."

For Reflection

- *How have you responded to Jesus' call to discipleship?*

- *Have you personally experienced some of the tensions that exist among Catholics today? How have you dealt with that experience?*

- *Do you think of yourself as a conservative, liberal or mainstream Catholic? How do you relate to those who do not share your stance toward the Church?*

- *What has kept you from being the disciple that you know you should be?*

- *Do you think of yourself as a missionary? How do you fulfill the Lord's command to make disciples?*

Closing Prayer

Gracious God, I have experienced the power of your love touching my life. Be with me as I try to freely give to others what has been freely given to me. Send the Spirit of forgiveness and reconciliation so that I may join with all my sisters and brothers in witnessing to the gospel of Jesus. Help me overcome my fears, transcend my ambition, and accept the cross in my life so that I may be an authentic and effective disciple of Jesus, your Son. Amen.

Notes

[1] *Pirke Avot* is a tractate of the Mishnah. The text above is taken from the English translation of Herbert Danby, *The Mishnah* (Oxford: Clarendon Press, 1933), p. 446.

DAY FIVE
Going Beyond the Law

Coming Together in the Spirit

If you have ever written a letter in the heat of anger, you probably regretted actually mailing it. We have at least one such letter from Paul the Apostle. He made statements that were harsh and unkind. Some of his fellow Christian missionaries provoked him and Paul let his emotions get the better of him. Unfortunately, Paul's words in the Letter to the Galatians have shaped Christian ideas of Judaism in general and the law in particular ever since. In this short letter, Paul uses the word "law" thirty-two times. All but one of these uses refer to the Torah in a negative fashion. Consider just a few of the Apostle's statements:

> ...[A]ll who rely on the works of the law are under a curse... (3:10)

> Christ redeemed us from the curse of the law... (3:13)

> Before faith came, we were imprisoned and guarded under the law... (3:23)

> ...[I]f you are led by the Spirit, you are not subject to the law... (5:18)

Now Paul was reacting to some Christian missionaries who told his gentile converts that they were required to obey the Jewish law if they wished to be saved. Paul thought the question had been settled when the leaders of the new Christian community met in Jerusalem to discuss this subject (see Acts 13:1—15:35). The conclusion of these discussions was that Gentile converts to Christianity were not bound to the law but were to observe those elements that made fellowship with Jews and Jewish Christians possible.

Defining Our Thematic Context

Christians often contrast "the Spirit" with the law. The latter's value was limited to a specific moment in the life of God's people. We Christians live in the age of the Spirit and are no longer "in custody under the law."

Matthew tells us that the first duty of a disciple is to obey—but what should we obey? For Matthew the answer is both simple and complex. The disciple is to obey the law. But what is the law? In Jesus' day, there was no single answer. The New Testament leaves us with the impression that it was either Jesus' way or the Pharisees' way. Actually, until the destruction of the Temple of Jerusalem in A.D. 70, the Pharisees were a distinct minority. It is estimated that only about ten percent of Palestinian Jews followed the Pharisaic pattern of observance. Matthew is most acerbic when he speaks of the Pharisaic approach to the law (see chapter 23). The sharpness of his words reflects the Middle Eastern way of disputation, which has no use for the niceties of a scholarly debate or the politeness of today's interfaith discussions. Matthew is being faithful to Jesus' approach to the law. While Jesus did not accept the Pharisaic interpretation of the law, he was observant in his own way. The Gospels never present Jesus as violating any of the commandments of the written Torah. Jesus expected his disciples to observe the law and, more than this, to go beyond the commandments. The measure of their gratitude to God was not to be circumscribed by the law but inspired by their experience of God's forgiveness and patterned by the needs of their sisters and brothers.

It is ironic that one group of Christians who recognize this are fundamentalists. They claim that the Gospels present Jesus preaching to Jews who were living under the law. He is not speaking to Christians living under grace. It is the epistles and the Book of Revelation that do the latter. The Gospels, then, are irrelevant to those who want to be saved in this age. There is only one way to salvation: Confessing one's sins and accepting Christ's death as atonement for these sins. Only those who make this confession and acceptance will be saved; all others will be lost. Most other Christians reject this as unreasonable reductionism. Through the Gospels, Jesus is speaking to us today. He is telling us how to shape our life of conversion and discipleship. The foundation of that discipleship is obedience. It is to that foundation that we now turn.

Opening Prayer

Loving God, send your Spirit to us so that we can discern your loving presence and your divine will in the law that is our heritage from your people, ancient Israel. Give us a generous spirit so that, following Jesus, we may go beyond the law in loving our sisters and brothers—especially those in need. Help us to appreciate the religious traditions of the children of Abraham, the first to hear your word. May our common commitment to obeying your will, as revealed in your law, become a bridge of understanding. We ask this through Christ our Lord. Amen.

Retreat Session Five

The Gospels reflect more than one level of religious conflict. First, it is clear that both the priestly and lay religious leadership of Judaism had problems with Jesus. The priests considered Jesus a threat to the accommodation they made with the Romans. The priests believed that they were acting in the best interests of the Jewish people since the Romans gave them a small measure of self-government and, more importantly, allowed them to practice their religion without having to participate in the cult of the emperor. The Pharisees found Jesus troublesome because he was a popular teacher who did not accept the "oral law."

A second level of conflict is evident in the early Church, which was developing its own identity separate from Judaism. As this was happening, Christians had disagreements with one another about the continuing significance for the law—especially for gentile converts whose number was quickly outpacing that of the Jewish Christians.

Careful readers of Matthew's Gospel will discern a third level of religious conflict that is unique to the First Gospel. Matthew accepted the rapid spread of the gospel among the gentiles. He saw this as a fulfillment of Christ's commission to "make disciples of all nations" (28:19). Still, he wanted the Jewishness of the Christian community to remain intact. At the same time, however, he sought to distinguish his vision of this "Jewishness" from that of the Pharisees. Matthew had to walk a very thin line to avoid abandoning Judaism while keeping his distance from a type of Judaism that was steadily gaining popularity in Palestine. Matthew's insistence on maintaining the Jewish character of the Christian movement ought to lead the sensitive reader to prayerfully consider the role of the law in the Christian life. At the very least, it can offer a healthy balance to an excessive concern for uniformity under the guise of fidelity to the magisterium. Matthew reminds us that the following of Jesus is more a matter of obedience—"right doing"—rather than of doctrinal orthodoxy—"right thinking."

The Gospel of Mark, which Matthew used in composing his Gospel, never uses the word "law." Matthew's introduction of this term in his story of Jesus' ministry shows that he considered it an important subject. The evangelist never loads this term with negative connotations as does Paul in Galatians. Most often in Matthew "the law" refers to the Pentateuch. Twice, it probably refers to divine revelation in general. It never refers to the Pharisees' "oral law," which Jesus rejected. Matthew reserves the terms "the tradition of the elders" or "your tradition" to speak of the oral law.

Matthew's references to "the law" make it clear that he valued that law. Like the religious Jews of his day, Matthew believed that the whole life of the people belonged to God. The law contains the requirements of the God to whom Israel belongs because of what God has done for Israel in the Exodus. They are not conditions necessary for Israel to have a relationship with God. God has already established that relationship by freeing Israel from slavery in Egypt. Keeping the law, then, does not establish Israel's relationship with God but maintains that relationship. The law is the revelation of God's will for

Israel and came directly from God at Sinai. The law is a gift from God, showing the people of Israel how they are to live in accord with their standing as the people that God chose. The law, then, is the link between Israel and God. Its purpose is to impart God's blessings to the people.

When the law was written down in the form we now have, it became the object of study and meditation. It had to be copied with great care—not a single mistake could be tolerated in any Torah scroll. When Judaism was developing into a religion concerned with individual salvation, the law became the source telling people what to do or not to do in view of gaining God's approval for eternal life. Disobedience brought with it great tragedy. Breaking the law meant death. Jesus shared this notion of the law's relation to a person's salvation. That is precisely the reason he calls for repentance. Jesus was convinced that God's final act on Israel's behalf was about to happen. The great day of the Lord will involve resurrection of the just and unjust for judgment (see Daniel 12:2). Jesus urged people to repent in preparation for that day of judgment. It is Jesus' call for repentance that implies his affirmation of the law's importance in the life of God's people.

Too often, Jesus is presented as someone who opposed the law and offered people another way to express their devotion to God. Jesus did not oppose the law but a type of interpretation that made it difficult for people to experience the immediacy of law as mediating God's will for them. Jesus spoke to a specific audience and geared his teaching style accordingly. Philo, a contemporary of Jesus, wrote in Greek for a sophisticated and philosophically literate audience of Jews living in Egypt. He used allegory and philosophical concepts in speaking about the law. The people at Qumran, a group of dissident priests, emphasized purity and separation for evil as they wrote about the law. The Pharisees and scribes gave themselves totally to the study and teaching of the law—something that most people could not do. Jesus did not study the law in the way that engaged the scribes and the Pharisees (see Matthew 13:53-58). This led the religious authorities to question his competence to teach and to request some sign of divine approbation. Jesus' audience was made up of ordinary people—not philosophers, not dissident priests, not scholars of the law—but ordinary people. Jesus spoke in plain words to plain people:

> At that time Jesus said, "I thank you, Father, Lord of heaven and earth, because you have hidden these things from the wise and the intelligent and have revealed them to infants; yes, Father, for such was your gracious will. All things have been handed over to me by my Father; and no one knows the Son except the Father, and no one knows the Father except the Son and anyone to whom the Son chooses to reveal him." (11:23-27)

Jesus affirmed the importance of the law by his careful observance. To underscore this, Matthew tells a story that none of the other evangelists relate: the paying of the Temple tax. According to Exodus 30:13-15, each male Israelite is to pay a half-shekel each year for the maintenance of the Temple. While Jesus implies that he is exempt from this law, he pays the tax nonetheless (17:24-27). If Jesus observes the law, shouldn't his followers? To emphasize this, Matthew notes that Jesus made certain that Peter paid the tax as well. Matthew also has Jesus affirm that doing God's will means keeping the commandments and keeping the commandments is the way to eternal life. Matthew has Jesus criticize, in most vehement terms, the pattern of observance exhibited by some Pharisees (chapter 23). For example, Jesus pointed to the irony of sheltering disobedience behind the law:

> [Jesus] answered [the Pharisees and scribes from Jerusalem], "And why do you break the commandment of God for the sake of your tradition? For God said, 'Honor your father and your mother,' and 'Whoever speaks evil of father or mother must surely die.' But you say that whoever tells father or mother, 'Whatever support you might have had from me is given to God,' then that person need not honor the father. So, for the sake of your tradition, you make void the word of God." (15:3-6)

Clearly this is not a criticism of the law, but a most radical affirmation based on the core of the law: the love of God and neighbor. Matthew has Jesus imply that the Pharisees were not at all observant, despite appearances. What Jesus did, then, was to restore the true purpose of observance: serving God and neighbor in love. The pattern of observance that Jesus criticized was one that only served to promote self-righteousness.

One problem that inevitably comes with the law is the temptation to casuistry. Here a person's imagination and creativity develop ways to do the least and still supposedly remain in compliance with the law. When Jesus criticized this focus on determining minimal obligations, he did so to underscore the extent of the law's demands. Quoting Deuteronomy 6:5, Jesus affirms the extent of the law's expectations, "You shall love the Lord your God with *all* your heart, and with *all* your soul, and with *all* your mind" (22:37, emphasis added).

Jesus, then, was demanding even more than the Pharisees were. Still, this demand for total obedience did not originate with Jesus but is found within the law itself. As Matthew presents it, the great flaw in the Pharisaic system was its concentration on the act alone rather than on the attitude that prompted the act. The irony was that the act could be in accord with the law and still be sinful because the attitude that prompted it was not love of God and neighbor.

Jesus' call for repentance flows from the failure of people to keep the law. The failure of Jesus' mission was due to the blindness of so many to their need for repentance. He was so disappointed with the lack of response he received in Galilee where he spent most of his time that he cursed three of its principal towns:

> [Jesus] began to reproach the cities where most of his deeds of power had been done, because they did not repent. "Woe to you, Chorazin! Woe to you, Bethsaida! For if the deeds of power done in you had been done in Tyre and Sidon, they would have repented long ago in sackcloth and ashes. But I tell you, on the day of judgment it will be more tolerable for Tyre and Sidon than for you. And you, Capernaum, will you be exalted to heaven? No, you will be brought down to Hades. For if the deeds of power done in you had been done in Sodom, it would have remained until this day. But I tell you that on the day of judgment it will be more tolerable for the land of Sodom than for you." (11:20-24)

Historical circumstances led to the growing dominance of the Pharisaic approach to Judaism following the fall of Jerusalem during the First Revolt against Rome in A.D. 70. The Pharisees continued to refine their system as they continued to reflect on the role of the law within Judaism. The Pharisees came to see the law as the central reality in their life with God. They believed the law to be authoritative because of its origin in God. But they came to see the law as more than the result of divine revelation; they came to personify it, believing that it existed before the creation of the world (compare Sirach 24:1-34, especially verse 23).

Liturgical practice reflected the importance that the law began to have for the rabbis. When the law was read in the synagogue, the reader stood on a raised platform so that before reading one had to ascend and after reading one had to descend. Even the scrolls on which the law was written came to share in the law's sanctity which was so great that after handling the scrolls people had to wash their hands before returning to secular activity. The scrolls of the law were reverently carried in procession before and after reading and stored in specially constructed arks. In today's synagogues, the ark is the central liturgical object.

The criticisms that Jesus had of some patterns of observance are echoed in the words of later rabbis. It is a serious mistake to believe that the casuistry and minimalism to which Jesus points were characteristic of Pharisaic Judaism or its successor, rabbinic Judaism. From reading Matthew, we might think that the Pharisees did little but trivialize the law and find ways of evading its observance while appearing to be pious. Even a cursory reading of rabbinic texts shows that the rabbis considered inward piety as the prerequisite of genuine observance. Their efforts were focused on helping people learn how to make observance possible in the circumstances of their everyday life.

Still, Matthew saw a genuine difference between the approach of the Pharisees and that of Jesus toward the law. To insure compliance to the written law, the Pharisees "surrounded" each law with prescriptions whose observance guaranteed that the written law would be kept. For example, the written law requires that people keep the Sabbath holy by refraining from work (Exodus 20:8-11; Deuteronomy 5:12-15). Since it was impossible to avoid all activity on the Sabbath, the Pharisees specified exactly what activities should be considered "work." They described the extent to which one could engage in ordinary acts like walking before they became "work." Building "a fence" around the law was the Pharisees' answer to the problem of insuring obedience.

But Jesus expected his disciples to go "beyond the law." For them, the law was just the starting point in their attempts to give expression to their love of God and neighbor. Matthew has Jesus describe this approach at the very beginning of his ministry. We know that section of Matthew's Gospel as "the Sermon on the Mount" (chapters 5-7). Review these chapters now as though you were hearing the sermon for the first time.

In the sermon, Jesus illustrates what he means by the greater righteousness that is to be a mark of his disciples. Of course, Jesus offered a few examples. He did not intend to provide an exhaustive list. What the disciples will do to surpass the righteousness of the Pharisees depends on the generosity of their response to God, the needs that they discern in the lives of their sisters and brothers and their creativity in meeting those needs.

The setting that Matthew provides for the sermon certainly resonated with his first readers. He has Jesus go up "to the mountain" (5:1). Mountains were the privileged place of revelation in the biblical tradition. Moses went up to Sinai (Exodus 19:20) to receive the law and Elijah returned there to hear the Lord's voice (1 Kings 19:8). Once on the mountain, Jesus "was seated" and he began to teach. This was the posture taken by authorized teachers of the law in the liturgical assembly. Later Jesus would refer to the scribes and Pharisees as those who "sit on Moses' seat" (Matthew 23:2). This phrasing told Matthew's first readers that Jesus was about to deliver divine revelation.

What Jesus does not do is provide additional

commandments for the people to learn and observe. That was the tack the Pharisees took and one that Jesus rejected. In the sermon, Jesus described the quality of the moral life that his disciples were to lead. Jesus wanted his disciples to probe what obedience meant in the circumstances of their lives for he demanded more than conformity to minimal demands.

Unfortunately, not all Christians have read the Sermon this way. A popular approach was to consider Jesus' sermon as providing "counsels of perfection," which only those specially called, such as monks and nuns, were bound to follow. The Ten Commandments were to guide the moral choices of the vast body of the Christian faithful. Matthew has Jesus address the crowds and the disciples (5:1) and certainly intended these words to speak to all who accepted Jesus' call to discipleship. Another way that interpreters have negated the value of the sermon for the Church was to consider the sermon an example of "interim ethics." Matthew provided the early Christians with the radical demands of the sermon because he and most other Christians believed that the end of the age was imminent. The sermon, then, was not meant for the long haul but only for a short time. Matthew, however, wrote for a settled community that was both urban and prosperous. That they were expecting anything close to an immediate end to this age is unlikely.

Some contemporary Christians have been so taken by what they see as the purposely exaggerated demands of the sermon that they have concluded that it was Jesus' purpose to drive his disciples to despair of their ability to shape their lives according to the sermon's values. Once they have abandoned all hope of fulfilling Christ's expectations, the disciples would then, forced by their failure, turn to repentance and faith. But how could Jesus expect people to repent of the failure to fulfill commands that were beyond their ability in the first place? Another way to absolve Christians from actually living up to the demands of the sermon is to regard its language as purely figurative, describing what people should be rather than providing them with imperatives regarding what they should do.

There is no question that the Sermon on the Mount presents the disciples of Jesus with a moral vision that is breathtaking in its dimensions. Still, it is important to hear that sermon against the backdrop of Jesus' dispute with the Pharisees and Matthew's dispute with both the Jews who did not accept Jesus as the Messiah and the Christians who wanted to abandon the Jewish matrix of their community of faith. To the Pharisees Matthew has Jesus saying, "I agree with you regarding the abiding value of the law. Where I do not agree is with your program of insuring that abiding value. You want to carefully circumscribe the limits of observance. I want my followers to burst beyond those limits. The only limit that makes any sense is the extent of their love for God and their neighbor." To those Jews who did not accept Jesus as the Messiah, Matthew says, "We have not abandoned the law. We continue to fast, pray and give alms as you do, but Jesus has asked us to go beyond the Law as we await the full revelation of God's sovereignty in this world." To those Christians who wanted to leave behind all vestiges of Judaism, Matthew asserts, "Jesus wanted us to observe the Law—not abandon it. He showed us how to fulfill the Law's demands in a new and exciting way. Still, it is the Law revealed to Moses on Sinai that we observe. It is, after all, God's revelation which Jesus came to fulfill—not abolish."

How did Matthew's audience hear him? For the most part, we can only speculate. Clearly, he did not convince many traditional Jews. The Church and the Synagogue, both heirs of ancient Israel's religious traditions, went their separate ways. It was a separation that had terrible consequences for the Jewish community once Christianity became the state religion of the Roman Empire at the beginning of the fourth century. Jews faced centuries of misunderstanding, libel and persecution from Christians who became estranged from their Jewish sisters and brothers. This separation harmed the Christian community, too. The Church soon began its preoccupation with doctrinal orthodoxy with dire consequences for its unity.

Did Matthew fare any better with his Christian audience? It is difficult to tell what Jewish Christians thought of Matthew's efforts. Perhaps they welcomed his words since they would have been looking for a way to continue living according to their ancestral traditions while maintaining their faith in Jesus as the messiah. Unfortunately, they left behind no written records to help us understand how they integrated their traditions with their faith in Jesus Christ. Archaeology offers little help since Jewish Christians did not develop a material culture that distinguishes them from other Palestinian Jews. Whatever Jewish Christian community existed in Palestine to the fourth century was totally absorbed by the Greco-Roman Christian community that inundated Palestine once Christianity became the Empire's religion. Political circumstances frustrated Matthew's hope of maintaining Christianity's Jewish identity.

What about us? The Church has long abandoned its Jewish identity. Or has it? The liturgical reforms following Vatican II produced a lectionary that has a far greater selection of Old Testament readings for both Sunday and weekday services than the previous lectionary. The liturgy of the Easter Vigil is shaped by a Christian reinterpretation of the Exodus story and the imagery associated with it. The priesthood is another important link between Christianity and the religion of ancient Israel. There is not a single person other than Christ himself that the New Testament calls a priest who has any liturgical role in the Christian community. The Christian priesthood has taken its shape from the priesthood of the Old Testament—something the ordination ritual itself suggests. But far more important is the influence that Christianity's Jewish heritage can have regarding the priority of the ethical dimension of religion.

The Sermon on the Mount expresses the abiding validity of the law, commends those who teach it and corrects those who would abandon it (5:17-19). At the same time, the Sermon urges Christians to not limit their obedience to the Law but to seek ways to express a greater generosity than simple obedience requires. The problem is that we Christians have been trying to evade Christ's call to a higher ethical standard. We have evolved a double ethical standard. All Christians were to live according to the Ten Commandments while only monastic communities bound themselves to live according to the ideals of Jesus in the Sermon. Certainly Matthew leaves us no clue that the Sermon on the Mount was intended for only a small segment of the Christian community.

The society in which we live is vastly different from the one in which Jesus and Matthew lived. It is not so much a matter of science and technology that separates our two societies. Much more devisive are the differences in ideology. We live in a totally secularized society. Religion is confined to a person's private life. What the Church and individual Christians can do in the circumstances of modern life is to become "counter-cultural." We need to live by the ideals of Jesus Christ so that the rest of the society can see that there is an attractive alternative to a privatized, secular approach to making moral choices. The Church cannot be turned in on itself, nourishing only its members. The Church must be what Jesus has called it to be: a light to the world and salt of the earth (5:13-15). People will then see the good that comes from a life lived according to the ideals of the Gospel and give glory to God (5:16).

A retreat is a time to focus on what is most central to our life with God. Matthew tells us that the heart of this life is how we express our love of God and neighbor. He reminds us of the gift that God gave us in the Law and then how Jesus has called us to use the Law only as a starting point. We need to take a close look at our lives and the moral decisions we make every day. Are we satisfied with fulfilling our duty, doing the minimum, meeting our obligations? Jesus calls us to go beyond the commandments.

For Reflection

- *When you think of "the Law" what is your first reaction? Why?*

- *Describe what you felt while you were reading the Sermon on the Mount. Do you think the ideals of Jesus in the Sermon on the Mount are attainable? In what areas of your life do you feel most challenged by Jesus' words?*

- *How well are you acquainted with Judaism? How might a greater familiarity with Judaism enhance your life with God as a Christian?*

Closing Prayer

Lord Jesus Christ, you call us to a greater righteousness, you challenge us to go beyond the commandments, you show us the way to greater love of God and neighbor. Give us a share of your Spirit, who can empower us to transform your ideals into the reality of our lives. We pray that through our efforts, your Church can become light for the world and salt of the earth so that all people can see our good works and give glory to God. Amen.

DAY SIX
Preparing for the Future

Coming Together in the Spirit

The popularity of "psychic" telephone services, astrology and the occult underscores the public appetite for information about the future. Some people have a psychic adviser whom they consult before they make important decisions. A few consult with the "spirits" to tap into their knowledge of the future. The response to Hal Lindsey's *The Late Great Planet Earth* shows that Christians take a back seat to no one in allowing charlatans to lead them astray. This book, which simply rehashes old fundamentalist musings about the end of the world, has sold more than thirty million copies.

Like every such attempt to see into the future, the fulfillment rate of Lindsey's predictions is in reverse proportion to their specificity. His most notable failure was his prediction that Christ was going to return around the fortieth anniversary of modern Israel's independence. However, the State of Israel has just observed its fiftieth anniversary. Lindsey explains the failure of his predication by claiming that God has given the human race more time for repentance. The author will continue to sell his books, psychic advisers will continue to see their clients, and astrologers will still prepare their charts because people want to believe that they have some key to knowing what lies ahead for them as individuals and for the world.

Many of Jesus' contemporaries also had a keen interest in the future. Indeed, Jesus himself spoke as if he believed that the coming of God's reign was imminent. But, like the prophets before him, Jesus warns his fellow Jews that the future will not conform exactly to their expectations. They too needed to repent. Their place in the future that God is preparing for Israel is not guaranteed. Only sincere repentance and faith can prepare a person for the future when God's sovereign rule will extend over all the earth.

Defining Our Thematic Context

Today we consider how Matthew wrote about that future. As we read what he has to say about the coming kingdom of heaven we will have to be cautious on two counts. First, Matthew is an heir to a long tradition of Jewish religious writing on the future. There are several features of this tradition that warn the contemporary reader against reading these texts as if they were exact blueprints of the world to come. Jewish speculation about the future was marked by faith in God's ultimate victory over the powers of evil, but the precise contours of that victory could only be expressed with religious imagination. Admittedly, the products of that imagination are often strange and bizarre in the view of readers today. That is what makes it difficult to appreciate early Jewish and Christian works about the end of the age.

Second, we have to put aside our expectations of consistency and logic in these visions. Their purpose is not descriptive but evocative. It is to draw out a response of faith and repentance. If we look for precision, logic and internal consistency in Matthew's vision of the future, we will be disappointed. If we read Matthew on his own terms, we will find ourselves looking to the future with the confidence that comes from faith.

Opening Prayer

Lord Jesus, you taught us to pray for the coming of God's kingdom. May that kingdom come quickly. May our love for God and service of our neighbor prepare us for the great day of your return. Keep us vigilant as we await your coming. Send your Spirit upon us so that we will be ready when you return. Come, Lord Jesus. Amen.

RETREAT SESSION SIX

When experience contradicts the religious beliefs of people, they often hold on to these beliefs with even greater intensity. Religious people may respond to contradictions between their experience and their beliefs by either denying the reality of their experience or at least affirming that what they are going through is not the last word. At the center of Jewish religious memory is a God who entered into human history to free Hebrew slaves from Egypt and to give them a land of their own. The same God raised up David and gave him an empire that stretched from Mesopotamia to Egypt. God promised that David's dynasty would last forever (2 Samuel 7:16). In Jesus' day, religious Jews wondered what happened to those promises. It appeared that God was no longer in control of history. Israel fell under the hegemony first of the Assyrians, then the Persians, Greeks and then the Romans. What happened to the God who led Israel out of Egypt with a mighty hand and an outstretched arm, with great signs and wonders (Deuteronomy 7:19)?

In reflecting on both their religious traditions and the experiences of their people, Jewish writers produced an amazing array of religious literature that tried to deal with the contradictions in the lives of the Jewish people. Some of these reflections were added to the books of the prophets but most were not accepted into the canon of the Old Testament, though they had a great influence on the beliefs of people in Jesus' day. This early Jewish literature affirms God's sovereignty over human events by asserting that God has known the future all along and has revealed the course of history to ancient seers like Enoch, Daniel, Abraham, Moses and Ezra. Through imaginative accounts of heavenly journeys and visions, these writings rehearse earlier history up to the time for which they were written, showing that everything revealed to the seers had come true. This was necessary to convince the reader of the assurances that these books gave regarding God's imminent intervention in history to make things right. God will come to vindicate those who have been faithful (as in Daniel 7:13-27) and to punish the oppressors of the just (as in Daniel 2:44-45).

Some of these visionary writings that scholars term "apocalyptic" describe preliminary events or "signs" that are harbingers of God's decisive movement to save Israel. For example, according to Malachi 3:23-24 God will send the prophet Elijah to preach repentance "before the great and terrible day of the Lord comes." The Book of Joel speaks about signs in the heavens: "the sun will be turned into darkness and the moon into blood" (3:4). Other visionaries predict a period of intense persecution or of great tribulation immediately preceding God's final intervention (Daniel 12:1) and still others speak of great wars between the Jews and their enemies (such as Ezekiel 38). Believers who die during these terrible times will be raised from the dead (Isaiah 26:19; Daniel 12:2). Some visionaries say that the wicked will also be raised from the dead and will be condemned to eternal suffering (Isaiah 66:24). Few of these texts assert that the final days will witness the appearance of a "messiah," a king from David's line, while most mention no such figure but speak of God acting alone without any human intermediary (see, for example, Zechariah 14:1-21). The Book of Daniel points to a "Son of Man" who will judge the righteous and sinners at the end of this age (7:13). The body of apocalyptic texts that were circulating in Jesus' day both reflected and shaped early Jewish beliefs about the future. In speaking about the future, Matthew follows the pattern set by Jewish apocalyptic literature.

The words that Matthew places on Jesus' lips as he begins his ministry are a call to repentance in view of the imminent coming of the kingdom: "From that time on, Jesus began to proclaim, 'Repent, for the kingdom of heaven has come near'" (4:17).

Among the last words that Jesus says in Matthew's Gospel is a description of a vision of the "Son of Man" coming in judgment:

> ...I tell you: From now on you will see the Son of Man
> seated at the right hand of Power
> and coming on the clouds of heaven. (26:64)

These two statements of Jesus frame the story of his ministry—a ministry that has for its purpose preparing people for God's final intervention in Israel's life. It is a ministry oriented to the future. Some people think of Christianity as a religion tied to the past. Jesus lived two millennia ago. The Bible is an ancient text. The liturgy preserves old ritual forms: priests dressed in clothes of the Roman period, candles used for illumination, and prayers and hymns from another age. Places of worship are decorated with statues and pictures of people who liveds centuries ago. The principal leaders of the Church are old men. Every thing about the Church seems to point to the past.

Jesus, however, was a young man when he began his ministry and he was a young man when he died. The Gospels present Jesus as trying to prepare people for the future—the end of this age and God's final movement in Israel's life. Everything that Jesus says and does is to help people ready themselves for the future because apparently he believed that the people he preached to were going to experience the coming of the kingdom in their lifetime, "Truly I tell you, this generation will not pass away until all these things have taken place" (24:34).

Of course, the way Matthew presents Jesus as speaking about the future is shaped by Jewish apocalyptic traditions. For example, Matthew has Jesus identify John the Baptist as Elijah returning as predicted in Malachi, "[A]ll the prophets and the law prophesied until John came; and if you are willing to accept it, he is Elijah, who is to come" (11:13-14).

Like some Jewish visionaries, Jesus expected a time of persecution and warfare before the end of this age:

> And you will hear of wars and rumors of wars; see that you are not alarmed; for this must take place, but the end is not yet. For nation will rise against nation, and kingdom against kingdom, and there will be famines and earthquakes in various places: all this is but the beginning of the birthpangs.
>
> Then they will hand you over to be tortured and will put you to death, and you will be hated by all nations because of my name. Then many will fall

away, and they will betray and hate one another.
And many false prophets will arise and lead many
astray. And because of the increase of lawlessness,
the love of many will grow cold. But the one who
endures to the end will be saved. (24:6-13)

He also pointed to cosmic phenomena whose appearance
will be a portent of the Son of Man's appearance as judge:

Immediately after the suffering of those days
the sun will be darkened,
and the moon will not give its light;
and the stars will fall from heaven,
and the powers of heaven will be shaken.

Then the sign of the Son of Man will appear in heaven,
and then all the tribes of the earth will mourn, and they
will see the Son of Man coming upon the clouds of
heaven with power and great glory. (24:29-30)

Following that judgment the unrighteous will be
condemned to eternal punishment while the righteous
will inherit eternal life in the kingdom of heaven. They
will sit at a festal table in the kingdom with Abraham,
Isaac and Jacob and, of course, with Jesus himself. Jesus
taught his disciples to pray for the coming of the
kingdom.

Clearly Matthew follows the pattern set in earlier
Jewish writing as he speaks about the future that awaits
the righteous who repent of their disobedience and
determine to live according to the law. The evangelist
believed that it was Jesus who is the way to the future. It
is Jesus who is the messiah, ushering in the kingdom of
God. Those who live according to the ideals that Jesus set
out in the Sermon on the Mount will find that they will
have a place in the world to come.

Matthew, however, does not confine himself to typical
Jewish apocalyptic forms in speaking about the future. So

many of the parables found in Matthew focus the reader's attention on the coming of the kingdom and how they are to prepare themselves for it. The parables of the weeds and the net assert that while the righteous and the wicked may coexist in the present, there is coming a time when God will judge and separate the two. The parable of the sower teaches that it is necessary to "bear fruit," that is, live in obedience to the word Jesus teaches in order to have a place in the world to come. The believer should not hesitate to make any sacrifice to secure a place in the kingdom as the parables of the hidden treasure and the pearl declare. Three parables encourage readers to take decisive action to prepare themselves for the coming of the kingdom since there is not an unlimited time available for repentance: the wedding feast, the conscientious steward and the talents. Finally, the parable of the fig tree warns that all the signs indicate that the kingdom is coming very soon.

Apparently, Matthew wants his readers to remember Jesus' parables as warnings that they need to repent immediately. One should not be fooled by the prosperity of the unrighteous since judgment is coming soon. In the meantime, the wise disciples will be ready to make any sacrifice for the sake of the kingdom. They can be sure that their sacrifices will not be in vain because the kingdom is certainly coming and all the signs point to its nearness.

While Matthew portrayed Jesus as preacher with an apocalyptic message, the evangelist avoided using some of the more problematic aspects of apocalyptic thought. For example, apocalyptic thought was so taken with the future victory of God over the forces of evil that it tended to give up on the present, thinking it hopelessly corrupted. Matthew does not share this view. He believes in the power of the disciple to transform this world by living according to the ideals of Jesus Christ. Also, the principal characters of apocalyptic texts are people of the ancient past who had visionary experiences that transported them into the heavens. Often these visions were so bizarre that an angel had to interpret them for the seer. (See, for example, Daniel 7-12.) Jesus was a preacher who went from village to village in Galilee and then to Jerusalem speaking plainly about the coming of the kingdom. In Matthew's story of Jesus, there are no bizarre images that need an interpreting angel to make their significance clear. Finally, apocalyptic thought was marked by a certain dualism. There were two kinds of people: the just and the unjust. Apocalyptic texts served to encourage and support the just in the difficult times that they faced. These texts held out no hope for the unjust: they were going to experience the rigors of divine justice. The Gospel calls all people to repentance. There is no one who does not need to hear Jesus' message. At the same time, there is no sinner who cannot be reclaimed for the kingdom:

> If a shepherd has a hundred sheep, and one of them goes astray, does he not leave the ninety-nine on the mountains and go in search of the one that went astray? And if he finds it, truly I tell you, he rejoices over it more than over the ninety-nine that never went astray. So it is not the will of your Father in heaven that one of these little ones should be lost. (18:12-14)

One familiar text from Matthew is shot through with apocalyptic perspectives although today's readers often do not recognize these. This text is the beatitudes (5:3-12). The form of these sayings is familiar enough from the Old Testament: "Blessed (or happy) is the one who...." This type of saying commends action that makes great sense. They urged believers to take what can be characterized as a conventional stance toward life and God:

> Happy those whose trust is in the Lord...
> (Psalm 40:5)

> Happy the man who is always on his guard...
> (Proverbs 28:14)

> For the Lord is a God of justice: blessed are all who
> wait for [God]! (Isaiah 30:18)

The beatitudes differ from these "Happy the one who..."
sayings because they commend attitudes and actions that
make little sense from the perspective of this world and
this life:

> Blessed are the poor in spirit...
> Blessed are those who mourn...
> Blessed are the meek...
> Blessed are those who are persecuted....

> Blessed are you when people revile you and persecute
> you and utter all kinds of evil against you because of
> me. (Matthew 5:3-4, 10-11)

The beatitudes reflect a world view of a community that
sees itself as persecuted and misunderstood. It gives that
community's experience meaning by relating it to the end
that is soon to come. When the end comes there will be a
reversal of fortunes so that the poor will receive the
kingdom, those who mourn will be comforted, the meek
will inherit the land, and the persecuted will enjoy the
kingdom of heaven. While the beatitudes guide the
disciples' actions in the present, they look to the future in
order to motivate the disciples to adopt the course of
action they suggest. To make this very clear, Matthew
ends the beatitudes with a saying that asserts that the
disciples can expect a reward for obeying Jesus in the
world to come:

> Rejoice and be glad, for your reward is great in heaven.
> (5:12)

Jesus spoke to a Jewish community in Palestine that had no immediate prospects for political or economic independence. Its freedom to practice its ancestral religion without interference was dependent on the whims of the Roman government. The high priest had to give his vestments to the Romans who held them when not in use. His freedom to claim them when needed depended on how well he cooperated with the Romans in preserving civil order. Pontius Pilate, the Roman procurator, set up an image of the emperor in the Temple area and outraged the pious who considered such an action a gross violation of the command against images. The Jews of Palestine naturally looked to the future for a reversal of their present circumstances. Apocalyptic language resonated with them. Jesus used this language in his preaching and Matthew preserved it. The evangelist did so not because he expected a restoration of Jewish political hegemony. He believed that the kingdom had already come in the person of Jesus. Like other Christians he was waiting for the *parousia*.

The term *parousia* is Greek for "coming" or "being present." Matthew uses this word four times. First, the disciples asked Jesus about the sign of his *parousia*:

> When he was sitting on the Mount of Olives, the disciples came to him privately, saying, "Tell us, when will this be, and what will be the sign of your coming and of the end of the age?" (24:3)

In his reply to their question, Jesus mentioned the *parousia* of the Son of Man three times:

> For as lightning comes from the east and flashes as far as the west, so will be the coming of the Son of Man. (24:27)

> For as the days of Noah were, so will be the coming
> of the Son of Man. (24:37)

> [T]hey knew nothing until the flood came and swept
> them all away, so will be the coming of the Son of
> Man. (24:39)

Each of these texts underscores the suddenness of the Son
of Man's coming. In other places, Matthew associates the
coming of the Son of Man with judgment. For those
looking to the future from an apocalyptic perspective, this
announcement of sudden judgment is good news since it
means a reversal of fortunes. The coming of the Son of
Man will mean the vindication of believers and the
condemnation of their oppressors. Though one often
hears of Christ's Second Coming, there is no passage in
the New Testament that refers to Jesus' second *parousia* as
such. According to Matthew 10:23, the Son of Man should
have come before the twelve apostles completed the
mission on which Jesus sent them. While the delay of the
parousia clearly troubled early Christians (they expected it
to occur during their time), Matthew thought it important
to maintain these expectations, so he highlighted the
apocalyptic tone of Jesus' preaching.

The one prayer that Jesus taught his disciples focuses
on the coming of God's kingdom and hopes that it
will come soon. Raymond Brown, S.S., offered an
interpretation of the Lord's Prayer (6:9-13) that explained
each of its petitions as variations around the same theme:
the coming of God's reign. The prayer begins with
petitions asking that God begin acting in the world as its
real sovereign:

> Our Father in heaven,
> hallowed be your name,
> Your kingdom come,
> Your will be done,
> on earth as in heaven.

The disciples are to pray that God's name be recognized by all as God takes control of this world from the powers of evil. This will mean that God's sovereignty be acknowledged on earth as it is in heaven where it is supreme.

Give us this day our daily bread.

This petition seems to be less concerned about the world to come than it is for the needs of people in this world. Still, the interpretation of this passage depends on the translation of the Greek word rendered as "daily." It is not the usual word for "daily." In fact, it appears just one other time in ancient Greek literature. Its meaning is unclear. Jerome himself did not know what to make of this word, translating it as "supersubstantial," a translation that did not catch on. The translation "daily" was just a guess. Of course, it has become the "traditional" rendering. This petition, however, is likely alluding to the banquet that is often used as a metaphor for the kingdom of heaven (see 8:11; 22:4). It is not a prayer for the basic human need of food, but for the realization of the kingdom of heaven when these basic needs no longer have to be met.

And forgive us our debts,
as we also have forgiven our debtors.

The early rabbis saw general reconciliation as an effect of God's final intervention in Israel's life. God will overcome the divisions that plague Israel and unite the people as they were when the covenant was established on Sinai.

And do not bring us to the time of trial,
but rescue us from the evil one.

The translators responsible for the *New American Bible* introduce the word "final" into the last petition to make it clear that it does not refer to the daily struggle with evil but that final tribulation whose days God must shorten if any human being will survive (see 24:22). Again, the insertion of the word "one" underscores the final struggle with the power of evil that will make the end of this age. Evil will not give up this world to God without a momentous struggle and the disciples pray that they may survive this struggle.

Every time we pray the Our Father we are asking for the final in-breaking of the kingdom. We are asking that God will hasten the end of this age and establish divine rule on earth, which will mean that the new age has begun. Admittedly, we all do not offer this prayer with the mindset characteristic of the first disciples. Of all the biblical motifs, apocalyptic is the most difficult for most Americans to appreciate. Our social, political and economic circumstances are so different from those who found comfort in apocalyptic texts. People who enjoy political freedom, economic stability and social standing are not looking for the end of the age that will bring a reversal of fortunes.

However, apocalyptic texts do speak to many Christians. Evangelical, fundamentalist and Pentecostal Christians, who expect the "Second Coming" at any moment, find in apocalyptic texts hidden messages that, if carefully and correctly interpreted, give the Christian reader the assurance that Christ will return very soon. Churches in the inner city, Appalachia and other pockets of poverty find in apocalyptic texts the same kind of consolation and hope that the first Christians did. This is one reason for the success fundamentalist and Pentecostal churches are having in attracting Hispanic Catholics. These new immigrants find themselves on the low end of the economy. They often have problems with the political system over their immigration status. They have little control over their lives. Unfortunately, the Church is not always as helpful as it could be. It is little wonder then that churches emphasizing the apocalyptic find Hispanic immigrants to be ripe for the harvest. Apocalyptic thinking is not as far removed from the contemporary scene as we might think.

Apocalyptic literature does have something to say to all of us. First, it focuses our attention on the future. Jesus came to prepare us for the future, for the coming of the Son of Man, for the coming of the kingdom of heaven. Jesus' message directs our attention to the future. Yes, it begins with a call to repentance and faith but Jesus adds that he is making this call because of the nearness of the kingdom (3:17). For Matthew, then, the future as it is presented in the apocalyptic language of early Judaism, should be at the center of Christianity—rather than at its margins. The evangelist challenges us to put the future at the center of our life with God. We believe that Jesus, by his death and resurrection, has conquered the power of sin and death. What we await is the final revelation of Jesus' victory. Now, we have but an inkling of what that victory means. The power of evil still has too much power over our personal lives and over our world. We believe that as powerful as evil may be, its hold over the world is coming to an end.

What are we to do in the meantime—as we await the final and complete destruction of evil? Are we to retreat into our personal concerns and abandon the world to evil? What do we make of the beatitudes as guides for the Christian life? What does it mean for us to be vigilant as we wait for the coming of the Son of Man? The answer to these questions will depend upon our view of the future. Matthew directs us to approach the future with hope shaped by apocalyptic perspectives.

We look to the future with confident assurance. Believers are not like investors gambling on the futures market. We want to hasten the day of Christ's return with our attempts to transform the world through the ideals of the gospel. To do this we will have to follow a course of action that does not make sense from the perspective of this world, but makes good sense from the perspective of the future. The beatitudes Matthew gives in chapter 5 of his Gospel are not meant to be an exhaustive list. They simply suggest a pattern for the activity of Christians who await the coming of God's kingdom. What Jesus assures us in the beatitudes is that no sacrifice that we make, no act of renunciation that may be necessary, no service we perform for God or our neighbor will ever be done in vain. No sacrifice is too small and no act of service too insignificant. When Jesus does return, he will take our sacrifices and join them to his own. His coming will complete the transformation of this world that we initiated through our living of the gospel. Jesus will then present to God a perfect world, a world that has been transformed, a world free from the power of evil.

This Jewish-Christian apocalyptic perspective from the first century had its counterpart among the twentieth century's political and economic systems. Ironically it was an atheistic system: Marxism. This ideology is also consumed by its view of the future. It calls for people to be ready for any sacrifice to bring about the end of capitalism, which it saw as an evil system that fed on the labor of workers without giving them an equitable share in the wealth that they created. Marxists were convinced of the inevitability of their victory over capitalism. "We will bury you!" was Nikita Krushchev's promise to the capitalist West. Less than thirty years after the making of that promise, the Marxist dream of a communist society is dead in Russia and Eastern Europe. Why? Part of the answer is the unwillingness of the people in communist countries to continue making the kind of sacrifices that their leaders deemed necessary for the triumph of Marxism. The lack of personal liberty, the economic deprivations, crushing power of the state were all too much for the people who simply refused to sacrifice any longer.

It is interesting to note that the father of communism in Russia, V.I. Lenin, once criticized religion as the opiate of the people. He meant that religion's promise of heaven drugged people into ignoring their suffering on earth. This allowed the upper classes to use religion to keep workers compliant. That is why Lenin was such a relentless opponent of religion. He wanted workers to be painfully aware of their situation. He knew that this would lead them to revolt against the capitalist system. Is Lenin's critique of religion valid? Does religion keep people from recognizing the economic, political and social causes of their suffering? Does it promise people a reward in heaven as long as they accept the suffering of this life? Is this what an apocalyptic focus does? Does it promise heaven to those who suffer patiently on earth?

The apocalyptic vision of the future does not intend to make people ignore their present. The religion that Lenin criticized is one whose adherents stand in the present and look longingly and expectantly toward the future when their suffering will end. In religion shaped by apocalyptic thinking, believers see into the future—their apocalyptic visions tell them what that future will be like. From that future perspective, believers can look at their present and shape it according to their faith. Believers, then, can be in control of their destiny. They can make choices that they thought were not possible for them. Rather than keeping believers from focusing on the present, apocalyptic thinking enables them to do so with the confident assurance that comes with faith: the future God will establish.

As disciples of Jesus, we must heed the call to pray for the coming of the kingdom, to be vigilant and to be ready for judgment. We look with confidence to the future because it will mean the transformation of our world by the power of good. May our commitment to Christ and his gospel lead us to make our contribution to that transformation.

For Reflection

- *Do you often think of Jesus' coming again? What comes to your mind as you reflect on Jesus' warnings to the disciples about that day?*

- *Can you think of any "contemporary" beatitudes—"Happy are they..." statements—that reflect the circumstances of our culture?*

- *What do you think Jesus was asking his disciples to pray for when he taught them the Our Father?*

- *What does your faith contribute to your vision of the future?*

Closing Prayer

Loving God, our Savior Jesus Christ has already defeated every power of evil through his passion, death and Resurrection. Send your Holy Spirit to empower us as we await the full revelation of Jesus' victory. Challenged by the ideals of the gospel, may we join with Jesus in his transformation of this world by the power of good. Let us be with Jesus on the day when he presents a

new, transformed world to you, thus completing what
you began at creation. We ask this though Christ the
Lord. Amen.

DAY SEVEN
Living Matthew's Gospel

Coming Together in the Spirit

This retreat examined some important motifs in Matthew's Gospel. To better appreciate Matthew, the writer, theologian and pastor, we should begin at the beginning, taking the time to read the Gospel slowly. The purpose of our reading is not to gain information—that is what commentaries provide. We are reading to seek the Person of Jesus, the messiah and Son of Man, who wants to give us a place in the kingdom of heaven.

It is essential that we submit to the Word's judgment on our lives. We listen to the Word; we receive it humbly and gratefully. We allow it to call us to repentance by convicting us of our sin. As we read, we are honest with ourselves, leaving behind self-righteousness. We allow the Word to speak to us rather than forcing that Word into our theological or religious systems. To insure that the Word can speak freely to us we do a continuous reading of Matthew rather than jumping from one favorite passage to another.

When a particular word or passage strikes us, we reread it several times. We do not analyze the text but listen to it. We may learn the passage by heart. The first goal of our reading, then, is to absorb the passage—to make it part of ourselves.

If we allow it, our reading will lead to prayer. Sometimes we will offer God words of praise. Other times the Spirit will lead us to the prayer of contrition. The text may inspire us to remember the needs of our sisters and brothers so we will offer prayers of petition. After we complete our prayers, we may begin reading again, thanking God for giving us the grace of prayer.

Defining Our Thematic Context

If we read Matthew this way, he will lead us to the threshold of God's presence. We will stop our reading, becoming aware of the mystery of God touching our lives. Such an experience can last a few moments to a few hours. When this happens, we leave Matthew behind and allow ourselves to become totally preoccupied with God. This preoccupation expresses itself in simply knowing and loving. Prayerful reading of the Gospel can lead us to rest in God's presence. Matthew, then, can become for us a guide in experiencing the God who inspired him to tell his story of Jesus.

RETREAT SESSION SEVEN

During this retreat we have focused on six motifs from the Gospel of Matthew, trying to see in them how the evangelist attempted to convince his readers to maintain the Church's Jewish identity. Each of these motifs is significant in Judaism and Matthew tries to show that they need to be taken seriously by Christians as well. These themes are: Walking With Jesus; Who Is This Man, Jesus?; Hastening the Kingdom of Heaven; Raising

Up Disciples; Going Beyond the Law; and Preparing for the Future. How successful has Matthew been in convincing us of his vision of Christianity, his way of understanding who Jesus is, his approach to following Jesus?

Among the values from Judaism that Matthew wanted the Church to maintain is the belief in the Scriptures as the Word of God. Of course, the Scriptures that Matthew had in mind are what Christians call the "Old Testament" or perhaps more correctly the "First Testament." Matthew quoted the Old Testament directly many times and alluded to it many more times. He saw the ministry of Jesus in continuity with the "Law and the Prophets," a first-century Jewish phrase referring to the Scriptures. At the same time, Matthew believed that Jesus brought the Scriptures to their fulfillment as no other had done or could do. The evangelist, then, saw Jesus as both the heir and reinterpreter of the biblical tradition.

Here is one area where Matthew succeeded in convincing his fellow Christians. The Church may have abandoned its Jewish identity but it did not abandon the Jewish Scriptures. There was an attempt in the second century to accomplish just that but the Church rejected this attempt. Marcion, a Christian theologian, suggested that Christians forsake the Old Testament entirely and read only an edited portion of Luke and the letters of Paul. Marcion believed that the other books of the New Testament were too "Jewish" in character to be used with profit by Christians. The Church condemned Marcion's views and there was never another serious attempt to suggest that the Church no longer consider the Old Testament as the Word of God directed to it and as essential to its faith and life.

Still, Christians tend to neglect the Old Testament because they believe that its religious message has been

superseded by that of the New Testament. For too many
of us, the Old Testament is little more than a history book
that traces the story of ancient Israel's election as the
People of God and its unfaithfulness to its covenant with
God. They see the Old Testament as basically a tragic
story and an incomplete one. It calls for the fulfillment of
God's promises to Israel in Jesus Christ. The story of Jesus
in the New Testament has made the Old Testament
"obsolete" as a source of theology, that is, understanding
who God is and who we are in relationship to God.
Matthew calls us to take a new look at the Old Testament.
He wants us to see the Old Testament as the Word of God
that stands forever (5:18).

A most welcome outcome of the Church's renewal
following Vatican II was the growth of the biblical
movement. Christians are reading, studying and praying
over the Scriptures with great interest and intensity. The
Roman Catholic lectionary offers a diverse selection of
lessons from the Old Testament for both the Sunday and
weekday Eucharists. This has led to a greater use of the
Scriptures—especially the psalms—for the nourishment
of personal piety. Christian advocates of social justice find
biblical support for their ministries in the prophets. We
need to continue this delving into the Scriptures. We will
find in them the light we need as we walk with the Lord:
"Your word is a lamp for my feet, a light for my path"
(Psalm 119:105).

Matthew's knowledge of the Scriptures was not
infused. It came through study. In Jewish tradition, the
study of the Scriptures is an act of worship, an act of
submission to the Divine, a prayer. The evangelist, then,
challenges us to demonstrate our love for the Bible
through faith-filled study. The meaning of the Bible is not
immediately self-evident, primarily due to the cultural
and religious gaps that separate us from the people who

first heard or read the sacred texts. Our study has for its purpose bridging those gaps. Once this is done, the Scriptures can help us shape our lives through the ideals of biblical religion.

The biggest obstacle to this goal is the view that study and piety are somehow opposed. Of course, they are mutually enriching. For the believer, study of the Scriptures is an act of faith and love—not simply an intellectual activity. The knowledge it brings is knowledge of Jesus Christ. Piety that is not grounded in that knowledge can become self-delusion.

Though Matthew was successful in convincing the Church to treasure the "Law and the Prophets" as the Word of God, he was less successful in shaping the Church's answer to the question: "Who is this man Jesus?" Matthew answered that question using categories familiar to the Jews of his day. Jesus was a teacher who gathered around himself disciples whom he instructed about the righteousness they were to have—a righteousness that was to exceed that of the scribes and Pharisees (5:20). But for Matthew Jesus was more than a teacher. Jesus was a prophet destined, like the earlier prophets, to be rejected by Israel (16:14; 23:34-39). Still, Jesus was more than a prophet. He was the messiah. Jesus was that descendant of David, destined to sit on the royal throne, whose reign will inaugurate the kingdom of heaven. Matthew also characterized him as the new Moses, the Son of Man and the Son of God. Each of these terms probes more deeply into the mystery of Jesus but each emerges from Jewish tradition nourished by both the Scriptures and other early Jewish religious literature.

Once the Church left behind its Jewish identity, a new vocabulary shaped its reflection on Jesus' identity. Instead of teacher, prophet, messiah, the new Moses, the Son of Man and the Son of God, Christian theologians began

using terms not found in the biblical tradition to
understand the person and work of Jesus. Among these
new terms were "being," "essence," "person," "nature."
These terms came from the Greek philosophical tradition.
Jesus was one person with two natures: human and
divine. Jesus was one in essence with God. As Christians
began speaking of Christ in this new way, problems
around a correct understanding of Jesus in Greek
philosophical categories afflicted the Church for several
centuries and were the topics of several councils: Nicea,
Chalcedon and Ephesus. Most of these problems could
have been avoided if the Church spoke of Jesus as
Matthew did, using biblical categories and vocabulary
without insisting on the precision that comes with using
philosophical categories.

While the controversies about Christ may have
abated, they have transformed the basic nature of the
Christian faith. They have made Christianity into a
system of "right thinking" in which doctrinal formulas
stated with precision became paramount. The effect of
this concern for doctrinal precision has been the
proliferation of Christian Churches each claiming to teach
"the truth." Within each of these Churches, leadership is
vigilant for any departure from "official" teaching since a
fundamental responsibility of leadership is the
preservation of doctrinal purity and unity. Ironically, this
concern for doctrinal unity has led to hundreds of
Christian Churches.

Matthew is, of course, concerned that we know just
who this man Jesus was. Instead of a precisely stated
dogmatic formula, the evangelist offers us a mosaic
whose individual pieces were drawn from Jewish
speculation about the ideal figures who were to be
associated with the beginning of God's reign over this
world. At the same time, Matthew reminds us that what

we think and say about Christ is less important than living by the ideals he taught:

> Not everyone who says to me, "Lord, Lord," will enter the kingdom of heaven, but only the one who does the will of my Father in heaven. (7:21)

In Judaism, doctrines are not as significant as obedience to the Torah. Matthew implies that it should be the same for Christianity when he says that Jesus cares less what we think of him and more about how we live in obedience to the divine will. The evangelist suggests that we examine our priorities as disciples. It is not that dogmas are a dispensable part of the Church's life; rather, the Gospel is not to be combed for texts to support doctrinal positions but it is to be lived in fulfillment of God's will. This is one of Matthew's strongest challenges to the Church and individual believers today: make your Christianity a matter of living rather than merely believing the gospel.

Admittedly, Matthew faces another formidable difficulty as he tries to lead people today to reflect on, what is for him, a principal motif of his Gospel: the kingdom of heaven. Matthew's goal was to offer a reinterpretation of a traditional Jewish belief for the people of his day: God was one day going to restore Jewish political independence and with that reestablish divine rule on earth. This is not an issue for Matthew's readers today most of whom do not resonate with the metaphor he uses to speak of this Jewish hope. In the democracies of today's world, monarchy is, at most, a relic of another day. Most do not even preserve it in any form, preferring a republican form of government. Still, if we allow Matthew to tell us what he means by the "kingdom of heaven" and accept this metaphor for what it is, we will find something of great value for faith and life today.

Matthew asserted that there is no need to wait for the kingdom of heaven; it has come through the ministry of Jesus, who has defeated the power of evil that had controlled this world for too long. The miracles of Jesus—in particular, his exorcisms—are proof that he has brought about God's reign over this world. Of course, one reason for the rejection of the gospel by most Jews in Matthew's day is that people hoped for a political restoration of the Jewish nation that would bring with it economic self-determination. The strength of this hope is evident from the two Jewish revolts against Rome: the first in A.D. 67-70 and the second in A.D. 132-135. Matthew wanted to broaden the horizons of this hope. He wanted it to embrace the entire world. He quoted Jesus as calling for the disciples to be "salt of the earth and light of the world" (5:13). His view of the kingdom involved more than the restoration of Jewish hegemony in Roman Palestine. He expected nothing less than the transformation of the world.

Here, Matthew makes an important contribution to Christians today. He will not allow us to confine our belief in Christ to a private, spiritual realm. For the evangelist, the kingdom of heaven involves nothing less than the transformation of this world through the ideals of Jesus, the authentic development of the moral values found in the law and the prophets. The evangelist believed that his fellow Christians could hasten the day of the final revelation of the kingdom of heaven through their generous response to what God has done for them in Jesus Christ. Matthew hoped for nothing less than the creation of a new world.

Matthew tried to convince his fellow Jews that the kingdom of heaven in its fullness will not come with one swift, divine stroke. The evangelist emphasized the role of the disciples in hastening the day of the kingdom's final revelation. Matthew does not give a full portrait of the original disciples, but it is clear that they were a diverse lot. Here is one issue that Matthew helps the contemporary Christian community deal with: the diversity among Jesus' disciples today. In choosing his closest associates in the proclamation of the gospel, Jesus decided not to avoid the inherent tensions that came with selection of a group that is not homogeneous. Jesus had a realistic understanding of the tensions of Jewish society in Palestine and he sought to meet people where they were.

Today both conservatives and liberals in the Church have a difficulty with the diversity that Jesus chose to accept. They find themselves drifting further apart. Both have to avoid the temptation to make absolute one pattern for the following of Christ. We need to admit that we can have only partial insights into the mystery of God. The first disciples quarreled with one another (20:24) so we should not be surprised that there are tensions among Jesus' disciples today. The key to keeping these quarrels within bounds is to remember that we belong to the same family. We are all brothers and sisters (see 12:46-50).

In speaking of the responsibility of the disciples Matthew is clear: the disciples are to obey Jesus. They are to obey Jesus as servants obey their masters—with diligence and vigilance. Yet the disciples are more than just students of Jesus. They become his true family. They will carry on the ministry of Jesus and will share his fate. They will also experience their vindication.

This is the ideal, but Matthew is very realistic in his portrayal of the disciples. They had their fears, ambitions, their disputes. Worst of all, they abandoned Jesus in his final hours. Why did the evangelist paint such an unflattering picture of the disciples?

Perhaps it was for our benefit. Jesus has called us to

abandon ourselves to him, to commit ourselves to the kingdom, to renounce all that impedes our total commitment. He reminds us that we have to take up the cross. Like Jesus' first disciples, we will fail. Matthew helps us to see that our failures do not disqualify us from discipleship. We can be rehabilitated by the Risen Lord.

Matthew offers us the key to making life in the community of disciples something that is life-giving. That key is prayer and forgiveness. There is no better way to deal with the tensions in the Church than for the disciples to pray together for Jesus promises to be with those who pray in his name. Only if the disciples can forgive one another can they carry on the proclamation of the Good News that began with Jesus' ministry. What the disciples have received without cost, they must give freely. Since the disciples have received God's forgiveness, they are to become instruments through which others can experience that same forgiveness.

The greatest challenge Matthew had in convincing his readers to preserve the Church's Jewish identity had to do with the motif of "the law." Matthew makes the abiding value of the law for the Christian life abundantly clear, but most Christians' attitude toward the law has been shaped less by Matthew and more by Paul. Some of the differences between the two New Testament authors can be explained by their different audiences. Paul wrote to his converts in Asia Minor and Greece. The vast majority of these were not Jews though some came to Christianity through their admiration of the Jewish emphasis on morality. These were the God-fearers, some of whom may have joined Jews for worship though they were not full converts (Acts 13:16). Paul insisted, over the strong objections of some other Christian missionaries, that gentile converts were not obliged to observe the law of Moses. The debate on this issue among Christians became acrimonious and Paul used arguments with usually harsh statements about the law (see his Letter to the Galatians). But Paul admitted, "[T]he law is holy, and the commandment is holy and righteous and good" (Romans 7:12).

In writing to us about the law, Matthew is careful to distinguish between an approach to the law that focuses on its obligations, which he identified with Pharisaic practice, and Jesus' approach, which involved going beyond the commandments. Focusing on obligations will lead to minimalism—trying to determine one's minimal obligations under the law and being satisfied with them. It also leads to trivializing the law by giving too much attention to inessential elements of observance and becoming obsessed with the minutiae of observance. Finally, the great irony of some patterns of observance is that they served to undermine the very purposes of the law (see 15:3-6).

Matthew sets out what he considers to be the Christian pattern of observance in the Sermon on the Mount. With several examples, Jesus showed how his disciples were to go beyond the law in their observance. Jesus made it clear that for his followers the law was simply the starting point as they attempted to give expression to their love of God and neighbor. The limits of observance were to be set only by the disciples' generosity and creativity in expressing their love of God and neighbor.

Matthew's teaching about the law certainly has value for Christians today. The moral question that we should ask ourselves is not "What is my duty in this instance?" or "What are my obligations in this matter? It is,

> How can I repay the LORD
> for all the good done for me? (Psalm 116:12)

The final Jewish motif that we considered in the First Gospel was the future. Matthew wrote to people who were keenly interested in the future because they had given up on the present as providing meaning and purpose in their lives.

Matthew tapped into a worldview that had become widespread in early Judaism—the apocalyptic worldview. Jesus' own teaching reflected some of the most important apocalyptic concerns, which saw believers as an oppressed group and sought to give meaning to their lives by relating them to the end which was to come soon. And the end of this age will mean a reversal of fortunes for both the righteous and sinners. Matthew believed that the ministry of Jesus was God's final movement into this world, so the end of the age must be imminent. How close is the last day? Matthew seems to hedge a bit. At one point in his Gospel, he has Jesus assert that the disciples will experience the end of this age in their lifetime though he also asserts that no one knows "the day and hour" but God.

Matthew wants us to look to the future with confident assurance. Jesus has already defeated the power of evil. What we are waiting for is experience in our personal lives of the full extent of Christ's victory. In the meantime, we give ourselves completely to the service of God and our neighbor, knowing that nothing we do to aid in the transformation of this world will be done in vain. We await Christ's *parousia*, believing that when Christ does come again he will join our efforts to his own and then present a newly transformed world to God—a world of justice and peace, a world in which sin and death will be no more, a world where God reigns. Matthew's apocalyptic touches urge us to look to the future as we prepare ourselves and our world for the coming of the kingdom of heaven—a coming that Jesus assures us is "at hand."

Was Matthew a success? Did he achieve what he set out to do? In one sense, the evangelist failed. The Church and the Synagogue went their separate ways and in making this separation, some Christians sought to rid the Church of its Jewish identity and heritage. Yet we still have Matthew's Gospel. He can still succeed by showing us how the religious traditions of Judaism can shape our life with God today. Matthew insists on the importance of the Scriptures for the Christian life. He underscores the priority of the Christian life over Christian dogmas. The evangelist speaks to us of the kingdom of heaven and how we are to follow Jesus and thereby join in the spread of God's reign in our world. Finally, he helps us see how our vision of the future can shape our present. Matthew does all by calling on the religious tradition that nourished his own life with God.

We stand at a decisive moment in the Church's life. We are in a position to put a final end to the anti-Semitism that grew out of the Church's rejection of its Jewish heritage. Imagine how different this world would be if we had followed Matthew's advice when he first gave it. But Matthew's advice was not taken. Shortly after Christianity was adopted by the Roman Empire, anti-Jewish laws were promulgated. Some of the Church's first theologians began emphasizing the discontinuity between the Jewish and Christian traditions. Soon this legal and theological separation led to distrust, libels and hatred. It was not long before this animosity led to expulsions, ghettos and pogroms—and then finally to an event the last century of the second Christian millennium will be most noted for: the Holocaust.

This moral outrage was perpetrated by a people with

a long Christian history. It proceeded, with few exceptions, without protest from Christians of other nations. Now there are some revisionists who would deny that the Holocaust even happened. We ought to give Matthew a second reading if for no other reason than to begin reparation for what some Christians have done to their Jewish sisters and brothers. The Second Vatican Council has begun a process that can lead to a confession of sin and a request for forgiveness by the Christian community.

We also have personal reasons for hearing Matthew again. He makes available to us a font of spirituality that has nourished the lives of millions of religious Jews for millennia. Jewish spirituality grounded on the Torah, nourished by study and worship, expresses itself by focusing on real people and on ordinary life. Its moral dimension is what makes it so valuable for Christians. Today Matthew calls us to reimagine our Christian life by embracing the religious tradition that Jesus called his own.

Shall we answer that call?

For Reflection

- *How familiar are you with the First (Old) Testament? How have you allowed it to shape your spirituality?*

- *In what practical ways does your vision of the future shape the way you live in the present?*

Closing Prayer

Loving God, our Savior Jesus Christ has called us through his evangelist Matthew to make this retreat in your presence. By the light of your Holy Spirit, we have reflected on who Jesus is and how he has commissioned us to be his disciples. Come to our aid now as we go forth to live Matthew's Gospel with hearts more deeply attuned to your coming kingdom. What Matthew has shared with us may we be generous, wise and insightful in passing on to those who seek you. Thanks and praise to you, Lord. Amen.

Going Forth to Live the Theme

The story of how Italian film director Piers Paolo Pasolini came to produce his acclaimed black and white film *The Gospel According to Matthew* provides us with a fitting way to draw our retreat to a close. It seems that the Marxist Pasolini was a "prisoner" in his own hotel room because the streets of Assisi were completely blocked by snarled traffic. Pope John XXIII was making an unprecedented visit to the city and the crowds had converged on him to get a glimpse of the beloved "Papa." Pasolini had nothing to read to pass the time away so he had to settle for a Bible conveniently placed in his hotel room.

The director picked up the Bible and read the Gospel of Matthew from start to finish. He was so moved by what he read that he decided to make a film that would portray the powerful Christ Pasolini had discovered. On a small budget and using only ordinary people rather than professional actors, he produced *The Gospel According to Matthew*. His Jesus is filled with urgency to proclaim the kingdom of God; he requires his disciples to commit themselves completely to that mission. Those who made the film and those who watched it were changed by the experience. As Thomas Merton later observed of this film, "For it was evident that the men who went through the experience of making such a movie arrived at a new self-discovery by identifying themselves with the disciples of the Son of Man" (*Opening the Bible*, p. 33).

May our retreat with Matthew open us to a deeper

understanding of Jesus as the Son of Man and of
ourselves as his twenty-first century disciples. If Matthew
himself were sending us forth, he would likely do so with
words taken from the Scriptures. None are more
appropriate than the priestly blessing from the Book of
Numbers:

> The Lord bless you and keep you!
> May the Lord's face shine upon you, and may the
> Lord be gracious to you!
> May the Lord look upon you kindly and give you
> peace! (Numbers 6:24-26)

Deepening Your Acquaintance

The following books and videos will help you further your relationship with and understanding of Matthew's Gospel.

Books

Gare, David E., *Reading Matthew*. New York: Crossroad, 1993.

Hare, Douglas R.A., *Matthew*. Louisville, Ky.: Westminster/John Knox Press, 1993.

Harrington, Daniel J., *The Gospel of Matthew*. Collegeville, Minn.: Liturgical Press, 1991.

Kingsbury, Jack D., *Matthew as Story*, 2nd ed. Philadelphia: Fortress Press, 1988.

Meier, John, *The Vision of Matthew*. New York: Paulist Press, 1979.

Videos

The Vision of the Gospels: Matthew (Rev. Michael Himes). Available from St. Anthony Messenger Press.

The Gospel According to Matthew (The Visual Bible). Available from Videos With Values.

The Gospel According to Matthew (Pasolini). Available from Palisades Home Video.

Matthew: The Mature Jew (*Scripture From Scratch*, Part Four). Available from St. Anthony Messenger Press.

Where Jesus Walked (Pilgrimage to Holy Land). Available from Videos With Values.